My Lucky Stroke

My Lucky Stroke

One Woman's Journey

to Manifesting

an Ideal Life

Laurie Freedle

My Lucky Stroke: One Woman's Journey to Manifesting an Ideal Life
Published by MAGGIE HOUSE PRESS
Denver, Colorado

Library of Congress Control Number: 2019900214
FREEDLE, LAURIE, Author
MY LUCKY STROKE
LAURIE FREEDLE

ISBN: 978-1-7329928-0-1

BIOGRAPHY & AUTOBIOGRAPHY / Women
BODY, MIND & SPIRIT / Inspiration & Personal Growth

Cover Design: Nick Zelinger
Interior Design: Brianne Smith
Editing: Alexandra O'Connell

QUANTITY PURCHASES: Schools, companies, professional groups, clubs, and other organizations may qualify for special terms when ordering quantities of this title. For information, email Info@MaggieHousePress.com.

A Memoir

This book is a memoir. It reflects the author's present recollections of experiences over time. Some events have been compressed and some dialogue has been recreated. In order to maintain their anonymity, in some instances the author has changed the names of individuals and places.

Dedication

I dedicate this book to my husband, Steve, who is kind and loving enough that my baggage was invisible to him. Thank you for reading so many iterations of this and believing in me. Your love carries me through the darkness and into the light.

"Opportunities to find deeper powers within ourselves
come when life seems most challenging."

--Joseph Campbell

Introduction

The first time I recall manifesting something, it was a human being. When I was five years old, I wished for a baby brother. I didn't know the word manifestation, of course, or even understand the concept. I simply knew I wanted a baby brother enough to make it happen. I wished for him every time I had an occasion when wishes are to be made—every wishbone pulled; each first star I saw; annual birthday-candle-clad cakes. At night when I said my prayers, I closed with, "And please let everyone be happy, except bad guys, and I wish I had a baby brother."

When I was seven years old, my mother became pregnant. I was extremely excited to be getting my baby brother soon. My mother and stepfather had five daughters between them and were unimpressed with my prediction of a boy. I was incredulous at their lack of faith.

When they started decorating the nursery and talking of names in the feminine, I couldn't stand it. Couldn't they see my baby brother needed the best boy's name ever?

When the baby was due, my sister and I went to visit my grandmother. One morning, she said my mother had called in the night. I said, "Oh, goody, my brother is here!" My grandmother was stunned by what she thought was my correct guess. But it was no guess. From the moment I made the first wish three years before, I knew it would come true. (Unbeknownst to me, the wish had come true two years before when my biological father, who was estranged, had a son when I was six. It seems my unknown stepmother became pregnant almost as soon as I made the wish.)

Perhaps it was a coincidence, and the silly invention of a child's mind, but it is a small example of many great coincidences, strings of synchronicity, and happenstance that filled my life. The occurrence planted a seed in my young consciousness, giving me the audacity to believe that what I wanted truly mattered.

In 2006, the movie *The Secret* changed how I thought about, and approached, life. The movie instructs the viewers on various ways to bring to themselves the things they want. I tried to approach life in the manner it prescribed, because I hoped to have a life with more ease and less stress. I decided I wanted to manifest a winning lottery ticket. It was the only way I could imagine I would have the things I wanted. Every week, I bought my ticket and I followed the steps from the movie: I envisioned myself winning; I saw myself checking the numbers and finding they matched; claiming my prize and living a luxurious life. I even planned what I would do with my winnings—how much to pay off debt and live my abundant life; how much I'd give to certain people; and what I would donate to various charities. Every week, after doing my envisioning, I checked my ticket and I still did not find myself jumping for joy at all the matching numbers. I will say I had an uncanny number of small matches—one to three numbers—but it did not answer my prayers or fulfill my lottery distribution plan.

I started doing further research on manifestation. I read several of the books about the Law of Attraction, and even played Law of Attraction affirmation CDs while I slept. I made vision boards with winning lottery tickets on them. No matter what I tried, I did not win the lottery, and I could not imagine the life I was currently living would bring me the ease I desired.

I couldn't see that there might be a new way of living and thinking that would lead me to the outcomes I professed to want. *The Secret* simply did not seem to work for me. I decided to put away the thoughts of manifestation, and put my nose back to the grindstone, determined to work harder.

I was putting my desire for a better life off in deference to the more commonly accepted idea that financial success and happiness were only attained by bearing the weight of the world on my shoulders, rather than allowing the Universe to carry the load for me. I occasionally had thoughts of how the Law of Attraction could work in my life, but I didn't concentrate any effort on it.

Over the next seven years, without really understanding what I was doing, I did manifest the ideal life for myself, which I still live today—a life where I don't have to work hard and I still receive enough money to live decently; where I don't need to subject myself to stress; a life where I can be healthy and choose how I spend my time and energy. It happened in ways I never would have predicted...or even wished for. It resulted in a life that was quite different than what I thought I was asking for. Perhaps the Universe had tried repeatedly to give me the life for which I was wishing, but I didn't recognize or accept it, so I was forced into a situation that was horrifying and inescapable. Once I adjusted to my new life, I found it really was what I had requested, and perhaps the only way I—the independent, hard-working, never-satisfied-with-myself woman—could accept a life of ease.

I continue to manifest the things I need without much effort, but with much wonder and amazement. I have learned some marvelously intense lessons along the way; for instance, accepting the gifts life gives you isn't always easy, but it is worthwhile; following your intuition can save your life and lead you in the direction of your Soul's Purpose; and life does not have to be hard to be abundant. I feel compelled to share these lessons with as many people as possible.

Here is my tale of how I manifested, and continue to manifest, the life of my dreams. It is full of starts and stops; perfect synchronicity and complete obliviousness; serendipitous realizations followed by not knowing an opportunity even when I tripped over it. It reveals the trials and tribulations of getting to my Soul's Purpose and learning, in retrospect, how I happened to attain it.

A Note About Labels

My first challenge in sharing my story and what I've come to know was how to refer to Divinity in a way that speaks to everyone. In deciding how to do this, I thought long and hard about the labels we apply to the Higher Power. Some say God, some Allah, some Jehovah, as well as hundreds of other names. Then there are those who believe in a higher power but don't really know what label to put on it.

For me, the explanation that strikes home was learned through yoga. God is described as a divinity found within the heart of every being. It is a universal power, which unites and uplifts us all, whether we believe it is there or not. The Yogic (also Hindu) gods portrayed in yoga are ways to visualize this energy, for those who like a visualization. Lakshmi is a way to visualize God when you are seeking contentment and abundance in your life. Ganesha, the elephant-headed god, is a way to visualize God when you are trying to navigate obstacles in life.

I feel the strength of a universal power operating in my life every day. It feels to me as if the many different names used for this universal power are all referring to the same energetic being. Therefore, I have referred to this higher power as the Universe. This reference is not intended to be exclusive of any name you may have, but rather to incorporate all.

I also refer to the Path, which I feel when I am aligned with the higher power. Lao Tzu referred to this as Tao, or "The Way" and many

Christians refer to it as "being one with God." Whatever it is called, it is a powerful feeling and a lovely, peaceful place to be—if only we can find it.

I'm not trying to convert anyone to or from any religion, and my book is not written to resemble any religious text. It is merely the story of how I found my path to being in unison with the universal power, which courses through all beings, and through whom all things are possible.

"*If you don't change your life*, you're going to die." This was the pronouncement of Melanie, my doctor, during a visit to find out why I was experiencing pain throughout my body.

"Well, we're all going to die," I quipped back.

"You know that's not what I mean," she responded, pursing her lips in concern. "I am saying you're going to die young and you're going to die horribly."

I was stunned by the bluntness of her drastic statement, but I was not really surprised by the content. I was numb to this, as I was to many things in my life. There was so much stress and so little rest; so much work and so little play; so much strife and so little harmony. I had learned to tune everything out and get through life while noticing the strain as little as possible.

I considered my lifestyle healthy—I was one of the most fitness-conscious people I knew. I worked out regularly and tried to eat well, when I had time. I was of average weight and fitness level. Everyone always told me how stressful my life seemed, but I thought I was managing that stress.

For months before the appointment with Melanie, I had a continuous, dull, aching pain throughout my body, and horrendous migraines. I was exhausted all the time, and couldn't remember important things, like how to get to my kids' schools. I made the appointment when the headaches became nonstop.

This was simply the latest in a long line of health issues, however. My recent medical history started with irritable bowel syndrome. Medication had been prescribed and, for the first time in years, I could have a bowel movement more than once a week.

Next, my allergies became so exacerbated I had to take antihistamines year-round. At one point, I had gone into anaphylaxis while going for a run. When the paramedics came to take me to the hospital, they found a woman with a blood-red body, eyes bulging out of her head, and a cartoonish voice, indicating a swollen larynx. "What did you eat that you are allergic to?" one asked sternly. When I told him I wasn't allergic to any foods, only pollens, he did not believe me.

"This can't be an environmental allergy. A reaction like this has to be to something ingested," another paramedic said, as he motioned his partner to raise the gurney. They moved me to the ambulance for transport. Allergy tests the next week showed I had severe allergies to every grass, tree, and weed that grew in the state, but none to any food.

The next diagnosis was Hashimoto's thyroiditis, which resulted when my own immune system started attacking my thyroid. This created a host of symptoms, including memory loss, hair loss, absolute exhaustion, weight gain, and the aforementioned general pain, for which I was seeing Melanie. It turned out my thyroid issue was more complex than what could be handled in a general practice office. The primary result of this appointment was adding another name to my cadre of doctors. I now needed to see an endocrinologist to help get my thyroid medication regulated.

The secondary result of the appointment was a lot of food for thought. I knew, somehow, I needed to do something to change what Melanie had told me about dying. I knew she was right, but I had no idea what I was supposed to do to change, and save, my life. How did I end up here?

I began life in Houston, Texas, as the first child and grandchild in a family full of grown-ups. My maternal grandfather had been the editor for the *Houston Post*. He was smart, serious, and adored his first granddaughter. I called him "Bandandy" because of a speech impediment. We had an invisible pet mouse, who lived under Bandandy's bed. His name was Marmaduke, and he ate "tadioca" pudding. Bandandy's wife, my step-grandmother, was a stern British woman. She was well-educated and had a sharp wit—and tongue. She thought American children were raised in a lax manner and tried to correct this whenever she had time with me. Of course, she loved me, but in a way that felt punitive to me. She wanted to be called Granny, but I secretly called her Granny Grunt.

My paternal extended family was quite different. They were simple folk, not highly educated, and very hard-working. My grandfather was a painter and my grandmother had never worked outside the home. They were quite serious about religion, and everything anyone did was examined against how the Bible said one should behave. They were conservative in everything—the spending of money, the experience of fun, and the doling out of affection. There was no doubt they loved me very much, it was simply a low-key kind of love.

My mother, Madeline, was a beautiful, intelligent, and loving young woman. She had a full-ride academic scholarship to a private university, which she gave up, becoming a bride at eighteen and a mother, to me, at twenty. I adored her, and I knew she loved me tremendously. My father, Larry, was an adventurous, charming, and impossibly handsome young man. He swept my mom off her feet (and everyone else he met, except Mom's parents) and married her when he was only twenty-one years old. He had his issues, but I was unaware of any flaws and worshipped him.

My sister, Beth, came along when I was two and a half. I loved her, but she was a "baby," so I didn't really identify with her as a person for a few years. Once she could walk and talk, she was my baby sister. Although I might tease her, anyone else had better not cross her, or they'd have me to deal with.

Daddy was an alcoholic, and the problems that arise with alcoholism caused Mom to divorce him when I was four years old. He remarried soon thereafter and moved to Atlanta. There, his new wife bore my brother, Bart, a mere four months before Daddy was murdered, by a "crazy man," as my grandmother told me. I was six years old at the time.

Mom remarried when I was five, to Glenn, my stepdad, who was my father from then on. He was a nuclear physicist—incredibly intellectual and logical. He was strict, with a dry sense of humor that I frequently mistook for meanness. He was a wonderful, stable provider, and he loved me and my sister as if we were his own. But he never made me feel loved like my "Larry-Daddy" did. He and my mom had my brother, Mike, when I was eight.

I was a serious child, studying others and looking for ways to be more acceptable, more grown up, more perfect. My pediatrician advised my mother not to start me in kindergarten early, but instead, to wait so I could be further advanced when I started school. He told her it would be important to me to be one of the smart kids, and he was right. I was driven to be the smartest and most competent wherever I was. I was self-conscious and, for some reason, never thought I was *enough*.

I went to school in a small town and did quite well. I wasn't the valedictorian, but I graduated seventeenth in a class of over 500 students. I scored in the ninety-ninth percentile on the SATs. I was going to be a surgeon. When I went to college, however, I found out there were lots of kids like me. I was no longer in a group where I was in the ninety-ninth percentile. I didn't do horribly, but I didn't excel. After my sophomore year, I decided I would not be able to get into medical school with my high B-average grades. I was not good enough, I thought, so I quit college.

Soon after, I married Scott, my high school sweetheart. He was a lot like my Daddy, without the alcoholism—handsome, confident, funny, and very charismatic. He could walk into a room of twenty strangers and walk out with twenty friends. He didn't do great in high school, but there was nothing he couldn't figure out how to do. He was a mechanical genius and could build or repair anything.

Scott and I were the couple everyone wanted to be. We were fun to be around, joking and laughing all the time. We loved getting together with family or friends, playing cards, shooting pool, camping, or any number of things. We liked dancing to country music, and when we two-stepped, people stopped to watch us move as one. We treated one another well and had a zest for life that others envied and revered.

While I was in college in the early '80s, Scott had worked for a moving company. The company model was simple, so when I quit school, we decided we should start our own moving business. Scott had signed a non-compete agreement, so we needed to locate our company where we would not infringe on his former employer.

Scott had grown up in Colorado Springs, Colorado, and wanted to get his parents back there, where they had been happier. It seemed the perfect solution was for us to all move to Colorado. Denver was the biggest city, so in 1985, at the age of twenty-one, we decided to head west.

On a preliminary visit to Denver to find a place to live and check what we needed to start a business, we realized the city was not nearly as big as we had thought. We were coming from Houston (the population of which was greater than the entire state of Colorado) and wondered if we'd made a mistake. We were starting a local-only moving company in a city that could be driven across in less than an hour. In our youth, though, we were fearless. We brushed off the concerns and never thought of the possibility of failure.

Despite a weakening economy, a city that seemingly was not large enough for the type of business we were creating, and our lack of business acumen, Mile High Moving took off within a few months. Within a year, we were quite successful. Although there was a lot of physical and intellectual work involved, and occasionally some quite frustrating situations, life flowed. We seemed to be floating along a path laid out before us. We wouldn't have ascribed the word manifestation to what we were doing, but our luckiness was uncanny.

The success of the company was far from alone in the list of things we manifested. Something magical happened whenever we realized we needed something. For instance, my eventual career in accounting was a series of unlikely events.

When Scott and I first started Mile High Moving, he and his father were the movers and marketers, and I ran the office. We knew businesses had bookkeepers, so it made sense for this to be my function. I knew nothing about the subject, so I thought a CPA should be able to help me—not actually knowing what a CPA was, except the "A" stood for "accountant." I looked in the Yellow Pages (the 1986 equivalent of the internet) and found an advertisement I liked.

I chose Simmons & Co because one of their clients was a large moving company, so obviously they could help me learn to keep books for ours. I called them and told the receptionist I was an owner of Mile High Moving, and I needed help with our bookkeeping. She said she'd schedule me with Bob, and he'd be happy to see how the company could help us.

I walked myself into this beautiful CPA office—large and sunny, with a view of the mountains. I sat on the other side of Bob's large, ornate desk. He was a middle-aged man, with graying hair and a kind smile. He asked how he could help me, and I replied, "I need to learn to keep the books for our company." He asked if I wanted to hire the company to do my books, and I said no, I just needed to know how to do it. He showed no signs of shock, disdain, or ambivalence at this silly young woman who had no idea how the world really worked.

We talked for a few minutes, and then we began an accounting lesson. Right then and there, he taught me accounting. He taught me about debits and credits, about expenditures, assets, and liabilities, ledgers and subsidiary ledgers. He led me through several example entries in the old ledger books he had pulled out of his credenza. (This was before personal computing brought us all the intuitive electronic accounting tools we have now.) I listened intently and learned quickly. At the end of a few hours, I felt competent to keep our books.

He ended the meeting, and I asked what I owed. He said nothing. I asked where I could get books like the ones he had shown me, and he said I could have the ones we had used. I thanked him as I left, ready to get started on my bookkeeping.

I did the company books for the following year, and when it was time to do taxes, I called Simmons & Co. I didn't know how to do taxes for a corporation, so I thought I would return the favor of the time the firm had allowed Bob to spend with me by hiring them to do my taxes.

I got an appointment with a junior CPA named Linda. I brought in my ledger books and went over what they contained. She asked if I had gone to school for accounting, and I told her no, I had come to Simmons, and a man named Bob had taught me. She looked at me incredulously and asked if I meant Bob *Simmons*. Well, yes, I guessed, it might have been Bob Simmons. She asked how much his time had cost me. When I replied "Nothing," she asked if he had done the work pro bono. I replied, "I don't know what pro bono means, but it was free." She told me his billing rate was at least $300 per hour. I was quite surprised and honored by the gift of this kind man's expensive time.

Another instance of this magic manifested a home for us. We had been renting a house, and our landlord decided to move back into it, so we needed a new place to live. Rental properties were getting quite expensive, and we found it would be cheaper to buy than rent a house. The big problems were that we had no credit history or money for a down payment.

Our real estate broker recommended we look for a house with a non-qualifying assumable mortgage. These existed in 1990 but were quite rare. They were the result of special loans to first-time home buyers, who then had to be convinced to allow someone new to assume the loan. The assumption was a significant risk to the original homeowner, who was liable if the assumer did not make payments. The loan also required the assumer to be a first-time home owner, and they could only borrow what was outstanding on the loan being assumed. Therefore, we would have to come up with a down payment equal to the seller's equity.

We happened to find the perfect house with the perfect assumable mortgage, and sellers who would allow us to assume their loan. Additionally, we experienced a surge in business. This meant Scott had to work twenty-one days straight moving households. It was difficult, but he made it through and the extra money we made was exactly the amount necessary for the down payment on our new home.

Our manifestation continued after the purchase. We had to make some improvements for the house to be livable for us, and we were struggling with the finances of home ownership. Afraid we'd gotten in over our heads, I put together a plan to see how much money we needed to pay for the improvements and get past this hump.

Voila! A hailstorm ruined our roof. We got a check from our insurance company that, after buying the materials and replacing the roof ourselves, resulted in a surplus of exactly the amount we had spent on the improvements.

These remarkable examples of manifestation were quite spectacular, and we also had small instances that permeated our daily life. They were mostly unnoticed. When they did draw our attention, we simply saw the coincidence, not the miracle. We went through life with gratitude for the things we had, without understanding what was in action on our behalf—the Universe listening to what we needed and giving us intuition, leading us to receive those gifts.

Within two years of starting Mile High Moving, we were more successful than we had ever dreamed we could be. We had developed our little business into something that could provide a very nice living for the two of us, plus Scott's father, and our two mover employees. The work of moving and packing was physically taxing, but things seemed to happen exactly as we needed.

When we moved our business to an office, we were exposed to different ideas about how business was done. The other tenants in the building started telling us how unusual it was for people our age to be so successful. Then Linda, who still did our taxes, told us how difficult it was to manage an employee payroll properly for the IRS. An attorney, from whom we sought advice, told us our youthful and casual appearances indicated to him we were not mature or successful enough to afford a lawyer. And some other "experts" told us how hard having our own business should be. We listened to them, instead of paying attention to how good our lives felt, and we started to wonder what we were going to do when we "grew up."

During this time, we unexpectedly started a family. Our son, Jake, was born in 1988 to two twenty-four-year-old parents who had no idea of what parenthood meant. This was the first thing we'd ever done that seemed genuinely important to us. We had brought this little person into the world, and we were responsible for making certain he was physically and emotionally healthy.

We felt we couldn't proceed through life in the easy-going manner that had served us to this point. We were, *gulp*, grown-ups now, and accordingly, we needed to act like grown-ups. Without realizing what was happening, we started to change into what we thought being adults meant. What we had observed from our parents, friends' households, movies, and sitcoms told us being adults was hard and serious work.

Jake was a beautiful, sweet little boy, who depended upon us to be good parents, and we had to do it the "right" way. We understood we needed to work hard, and life was going to be more difficult. And just like that, life suddenly became hard.

Our work seemed more problematic and less rewarding than it had previously. Scott grew dissatisfied with doing most of the physical work of the moving company himself. Our customers, who used to adore him and treat him very well, suddenly said and did incredibly rude and condescending things to him.

"Do you know how many bones you have in your hand?" a customer, who was a former drill sergeant, asked him one day. When he said no, she told him it didn't matter, because she would break every one of them if he damaged any of her belongings.

I also became disenchanted—with being stuck at the office, splitting my time between caring for Jake and doing the office tasks. We had lost track of the Path upon which we could navigate difficulties and find the changes that produced ease.

We decided to give up on Mile High Moving. Scott wanted to go to college, so I looked for a job that used the skills I'd learned in doing the company bookkeeping.

At twenty-six, I found myself as an accounts payable clerk working for Winfrow Industries (WI), a multi-billion-dollar, multi-division company. I had discovered my niche—accounting made absolute sense to me. Working for one of the largest employers in the state, I naturally had a much more formal and intricate accounting system to learn than my simple ledgers. But I put my nose to the grindstone. I had a wonderful co-worker, who helped me understand the system, my capabilities, and even life itself. She served as a great mentor and encouraged me to take accounting classes at the local community college.

As Scott and I burrowed deeper into adulthood, we decided we wanted another child before we were "too old." I got pregnant right away, and Megan was born in 1993, five years after her brother, to her ancient parents of twenty-nine. She was an easy baby, and our family seemed complete. Suddenly, we were not only parents, we had two children and were almost *thirty* years old!

Now, things were getting seriously grown-up, and as we expected, life got even harder.

I'm not saying our life was awful, or even worse than the lives of other people we knew. We had the normal hecticness of balancing day care, kids' activities, family time, time for romance, work, and school. Scott was going to college and struggling to find part-time work that didn't interfere with his studies. I was working full-time and attending school part-time for my accounting degree. While finances were tight for us, we were making ends meet.

But we had been accustomed to being on the Path, to being attuned to the Universe, and having lost track of it, we struggled. Somewhere, deep inside of us, we knew life shouldn't need to be so rough, but we ignored the quiet voice, and listened to the external stories about how hard being an adult is.

We still had some synchronicity and manifestation at work in our lives. At one point, Scott wanted to quit his part-time job and concentrate more on his education. I sat down and worked the numbers over. If we cut out a few luxury expenditures, we would need $400 per month more than my salary at the time. I had recently changed jobs and couldn't very well apply for a promotion. I told Scott if he quit his job, we would need to find a way to make $400 more per month.

Two weeks later, WI's personnel division sent me a letter. They had looked at my job description and decided my job was misclassified. It would be reclassified, and the result would be a change in salary. I would be receiving exactly a $400-per-month raise! It was a complete surprise to me, as I did not initiate this action with WI, but apparently I did initiate it with the Universe!

Most of our manifestations took a toll, though. Generally, we'd need more money for something, and soon, a job would become available for which I was perfectly prepared. I would apply and get it, but there was a huge increase in responsibilities and stress (not commensurate with the pay increase). Or we'd get a windfall, only to have something happen that required exactly that amount of money. It seemed there was always a price to pay for the good things we received.

For instance, I took a lateral transfer for a job that had more potential for promotion. When I started work, I realized my new boss, John, was a complete burnout case. He came to work around nine or ten o'clock in the morning, took a two-hour lunch, and left by three-thirty. He was the agency controller, but had no idea how to log into our accounting system. He often approved purchases that were clearly against the fiscal rules, and plain old-fashioned good sense. With his constant absence, I, with a whopping eighteen months of experience as an accounting technician, became the lead accountant for the agency.

Doing both my job and John's was horrendously stressful, and if that wasn't bad enough, he became hostile toward me. Two weeks after Megan was born, I came back to work, conditional on being able to work part-time, some in the office and some from home. I felt I needed to do this because there was no way I could trust John to run the office by himself. He'd already completely messed up a huge entry in our year-end reporting. Within a week of my coming back to work, he had the nerve to question my leave usage, and tell me he might have to end my freedom to work at home.

One night, I dreamt he came into my office wearing a military uniform (he had been in the armed forces in his youth), found me hiding under my desk, and shot me. I wrote a message to Scott in my own blood.

When I told John about this dream, I thought he'd be shocked or horrified I would dream such a thing about him. Instead, he said, "Wow! That's interesting because I had a weird dream last night, too. I was back in the service. I had a job to do, but I couldn't get it done." My nightmare at home reflected the nightmarish nature of my workdays.

They say if you throw a frog into boiling water, it will jump out, but if you put him in a warm pot of water and gradually increase the temperature until the water boils, he will sit there placidly and die. Throughout these years, the needs of my family grew. As I managed to provide no matter what, I took on increasingly demanding jobs while trying to be the perfect mother and wife. The water was getting hotter and hotter and I was too busy to jump out.

Ultimately, I began to feel pulled from all sides—I remember wishing there was one single person in my life who didn't need 100 percent of what I had to give. The stress, the increasing demands, the apparent obliviousness of my family and co-workers to the strain of my life, all wore on me. I started having migraines. I began to perceive I was neglected, taken advantage of, and mistreated. (I was the frog, suddenly realizing the water was boiling, and I was trying to assess blame for who had been turning up the heat.)

Scott was experiencing a different kind of stress. He was a part-time student and stay-at-home dad. School was difficult for him, and he worked laboriously on his homework. In addition, in the late '90s, it was unheard of for a man to be the stay-at-home parent, and in his machismo Italian upbringing, it was an oddity. To make matters worse, his father, with whom he was very close, had passed away. In reaction, Scott withdrew completely into his roles as student and father, leaving me feeling alone in my battleground of work, motherhood, and being a wife to someone who didn't seem to know I existed.

Our marriage crumbled under the pressure. After several years of struggling with feelings of rejection, I couldn't handle it anymore. One day, after we had a big fight (a rarity in the first twelve years of our marriage), I simply could not stand it one more day.

I calmly said, "I don't want to do this anymore."

"Do what?" he asked.

"This—be in a relationship with someone who doesn't love me and work so hard when no one cares. I don't want to be with you. If I'm going to be lonely, I would rather be alone."

Everyone in our lives—including the two of us—was stunned. We had appeared to be the epitome of the perfect couple. In fact, the only problem with our relationship was we had "grown up" too much. Our lives were so stressful. We had no time or energy to take care of ourselves or one another.

During the years after the divorce, I continued to demand more and more from myself in all areas of life, especially work. I was rewarded with increasingly important jobs, more money, and disproportionately more stress.

I never asked myself why I applied for these increasingly difficult jobs. I had plenty of money to afford a good life for me and my children. I enjoyed many of my less stressful jobs, but I always applied for promotions when they came up. I suppose it was the fallacy of the American Dream that compelled me. I needed to make more money because I was supposed to want to make more money, and with more money came more, and harder, work.

In 2003, I was promoted to Chief Financial Officer for the facilities division of WI, a billion-dollar-a-year segment of the company. The job was incredibly stressful and demanding of my time. I ate on the run, inhaling whatever fast food I could find.

I exercised most days, because everyone knows, exercise relieves stress. But while I exercised, I was trying to find the answers to nerve-racking problems from work and home. I worked more than sixty hours per week. I stayed at the office later the days Jake and Megan were with Scott, but I had a policy of leaving by 6:00 p.m. (a ten-hour day) on days when they were with me. I rushed home and put on my "perfect mom" hat and did my best to be present and pleasant for my children. I slept an average of four hours per night. My heart raced constantly, and I couldn't relax. Ever.

My turning point came one morning at work during "leadership week." Two days per month, we had a meeting with the Leadership Committee, the division's decision-making body. The week in which these two days fell could have as easily been dubbed Hell Week. It was incredibly hectic due to the large amount of information that had to be gathered; the data that had to be crunched; the presentations that had to be created; the executive management approval that had to be gleaned; and the printing that had to be done in time for the meeting.

On this early morning, I stood in front of Trish, my assistant, coiffed and clad in my all-business navy suit, and coiled for action like a compressed spring. I was telling Trish that the presentation she had sent to the print shop last night needed to be stopped, because the director had asked for a last-minute change (which was not unusual). I needed 150 copies of the newly-edited packet ready in thirty minutes, when my presentation would begin.

At this point, someone from accounting approached with news. A six-figure check had sat in their safe for a year and was now invalid. Payments from this particular company were notoriously difficult to come by, and the fact that the money was owed was no guarantee that payment would be made again.

"How in the world could such a thing have happened?!" I exclaimed, willing myself not to scream at this messenger.

"I d-d-don't know," the meek accountant almost whispered.

"Well, I can't deal with this right now. Trish will set a meeting for the Controller to discuss this with Doug."

The accountant scurried off down the hall. My brain was buzzing with the added level of stress this information brought. As I resumed my discussion with Trish, I grasped my chest. I stopped mid-sentence with wide eyes and more intensity than the conversation called for.

"Are you okay?" Trish looked extremely concerned.

"Yes, but I have this horrible pain in my chest," I said, closing my eyes, willing the pain to stop.

"Oh my God, are you having a heart attack? Should I call an ambulance?"

Through clenched jaws, I said, rather calmly, "I can't be having a heart attack, I have to address Leadership in twenty-five minutes!" and I strode off to my office to collect my wits before facing the public meeting.

The pain relented, and I got through the meeting, not really thinking about the likelihood of a heart attack. I never gave it a second thought. But after the trauma of Hell Week subsided, I noticed the continued presence of the buzzing in my head. This wasn't a literal sound, but more of a feeling. It was like an electrical storm was taking place inside my brain, with lightning bolts chasing themselves around the small area encased by my skull. Try as I might, I could not calm this storm. I sat and closed my eyes, then started deep breathing. I worked out. I got a massage. I told myself to calm down, but nothing helped.

A few weeks later, I was tidying up my desk at home when I had a vision. In my arms, I was cradling a little bundle in a baby blanket. I looked down and pulled the blanket back, and there was my brain. The message was crystal clear—I needed to take care of my brain—to baby it to be exact!

I started paying more attention to the way my life felt, acknowledging the tension. It became obvious: I needed to change something, somehow, to reduce my stress. But I didn't know what I could possibly do differently. My family depended on me to provide for them. The people I worked with depended on me to keep everything straight there, managing increasing workloads while requests for new personnel were denied. I liked my job, was proud of the work my division did, and enjoyed the reputation and image I had attained through all my hard work. What I knew of the world was this: you must work hard to deserve a good life. I had no desire to change to a *less good* life.

As I began paying attention to my brain and body, I started to realize something big was awry. I made a doctor's appointment to start figuring out what was wrong with me.

I told Melanie of the pain and the migraines; the chest pain on leadership meeting day; and the total exhaustion. She put her hand on my shoulder and said, "My God! You are so tense! You need to call off work and get a massage."

"I don't have time today."

"If you don't change your life, you're going to die!" she replied.

I had no idea what I was supposed to do with this information, so I did nothing. I stored the conversation away in the back of my brain and carried on.

But carrying on was not so easy, because now I had the metaphor of my brain as a baby. Whenever I was stressed, the vision would come forward. I would try to soothe the baby brain. In my imagination, I would coo to it, and say, "It's okay. It's okay. Shhhhhh. I'll take care of you," while it cried and fussed. I knew I had to figure out what "I'll take care of you" meant.

Meanwhile, work was the same as always, but noticing it, and relating it to my crying brain, made it feel different. I cut my hours back, refusing to regularly work more than fifty hours per week. I started taking a lunch break and getting a monthly massage. I tried to keep my mind free when I worked out, and I persisted in pushing issues from my job out of my home life. But the calm I was trying to enforce in my off-hours was not enough to offset the anxiety I experienced the other fifty or so hours per week.

My job started to suffer. I made mistakes, some of them big, and my weary mind couldn't fathom what I was supposed to do. Defeated by the insurmountable workload, the exhaustion, and the insistent crying of my infantile brain, I decided to find another job. Maybe there would be something in a similar pay range with a bit less stress, making it possible to rejuvenate myself.

I applied for several jobs that would be drastically less stress. Of course, they were also drastically less pay. Then a friend recommended a job to me. I applied for, and got, the job as the CFO of a municipal water utility. This was another big job, but I was certain I was moving to something less demanding than where I was. I didn't think anything could possibly be worse. I was wrong.

Upon starting the new job, I found my position was caught in limbo. The head of the water utility, Paul, was working with the mayor to try to create a utility that was independent of the city government. The city manager and the city council did not like this idea. My job was to support the water utility, working closely with Paul. But I officially reported to Jim, the city finance director, whom I saw infrequently. On a day-to-day basis, I created finance plans and work products as directed by Paul.

I was learning a vast new world of finance, which was very fun. I had a small staff, who was eager to please me. We created very impressive finance plans and Paul was pleased with the work.

But when I met with Jim, he would not have been apprised of some new direction Paul and the mayor had decided to take. He was furious about what I had prepared, saying it was not the direction the City Council was going. I found myself stuck in the middle of a power struggle, in a no-win situation.

A few months into this job, I went on a family vacation at the beach with my mom, stepdad, siblings, and Megan (Jake was on a school trip). A work deadline had been advanced right before my departure. When I planned the vacation, the deadline was weeks after my trip, but Paul now needed my work product complete the day after I was returning to work. Therefore, I needed to work while I was on vacation.

It seemed immaterial, as I had worked on vacations many times—hard work was part of life, and vacation was no exception. I got up every morning by 5:00 a.m. and hammered away at my laptop until everyone else was ready to head down to the beach, around ten. I hung out with my family, and then when we went back up to our condos for lunch, I'd pull out my laptop again and see what revisions Paul had to the items I had sent to him earlier. After a couple of hours of toiling, I'd submit my new products and magically appear on the beach, joining my family and thinking no one was the wiser about the amount of time I was working.

On the fourth day of this "vacation," then eleven-year-old Megan said, "Mom, if I see you with that laptop one more time, I'm going to throw it off the balcony! You need to relax and be on vacation."

I was stunned. She never spoke to me in this manner. But more importantly, I realized she was right! At my noontime check in, I emailed Paul, saying I was going to take the rest of my vacation off. For the first time in years, I had three days of relaxation, spending time with family, totally enjoying life. It was a glorious departure from pretending to relax and enjoy myself in between anxiety-filled interludes of work, and it was an amazing reminder of what vacation—or maybe life—should really be.

On the last full day of our trip, I went for a walk on the beach with Megan and she expressed her confusion. "I thought this new job was supposed to be less stressful. It seems worse to me."

"You're right," I answered, "but I don't know what to do about it."

"I think you need a job where there is nothing to do when your day is over."

I tried to imagine such a job. "When I was a waitress, I didn't bring work home. But I don't think we could live on what I would make as a waitress. Can you think of another job like that?"

"Being a massage therapist would be nice. It seems really relaxing, and you'd be helping people feel better."

I remembered a friend at work who had gone to massage school and gave me massage now and then. Megan was right about it not requiring me to work during off-hours. I wondered if I could possibly be a massage therapist. When I pictured myself doing massage, I had a blissful, peaceful feeling. I filed this information away for perusal later.

The next morning, I strolled on the beach alone before we left. The walk was peaceful, insightful, and informative. On the plane home, I decided to write about it, and here is what I penned in my journal:

At the end of my morning walk, I felt an almost religious affinity with the ocean. Just watching, hearing, feeling it was like worshipping. The sound of the waves seemed to share with me the sea's wisdom and energy. The waves coming in brought insight and when they went out, they took away my confusion and self-doubt. The ocean told me how its destiny and path are not set by the boats which float along it. It doesn't need them, or the shore, to set its course. The waves set the course, and the rest conform, fight against, or go with, the tides. The ocean doesn't care. It is concerned only with its own ebb and flow; moving what it can, flowing around what it cannot. Always setting its own direction. As I finished my walk, I thanked the ocean for sharing its secrets with me. I feel more grounded and whole than I ever have before. Life is good.

In reading over my stream-of-consciousness writing, I knew I was, metaphorically, a boat on the ocean. I thought back to when I had allowed myself to float along, manifesting clear skies and smooth sailing, plotting the course to my destination with ease and grace.

Somewhere along the line, I had stopped steering my boat and started struggling to move the ocean itself. I had started expecting, and receiving, stormy weather, which made the journey difficult to manage. I was fighting a losing battle. I should simply roll with the tides and keep myself afloat, navigating my way in concert with the ocean. Instead, I was railing against it. The more I tried to control the ocean, the less I controlled my boat. There was something bigger at work in my life than I was acknowledging. The ocean—the Universe—wanted to lift me up and take me where I needed to go, but I kept telling it I wanted to struggle and fight, so I got rough seas and storms.

Upon my return to the office, I found Paul had worked with a member of my staff to tidy up the final details of the huge sum of work I had done over vacation. Then, he had attempted to meet with Jim about presenting the work to the City Council. He received the same tongue-lashing I had been getting for months about the inappropriate direction the presentation was taking. When he expressed to me how difficult Jim was to deal with, I thought, *Welcome to my world!* and smiled smugly.

During my second week back, I had an appointment with the endocrinologist to whom Melanie had referred me. I was continuing treatment for Hashimoto's thyroiditis, and the results of one of my routine blood tests prompted the doctor to suggest a test for rheumatoid arthritis. She said I had many of the markers for the disease. I was horrified to think I could have another autoimmune disease. I told her I would not do the test. I could not handle the thought of another disease; I loathed the idea of taking more drugs; and I preferred ignorance.

On the way home from the appointment, the prediction of my imminent death from my earlier visit with Melanie echoed in my head. I was thirty-nine years old when the initial prognosis was given. I hadn't done enough about the warning and, now, at forty-two, the words rang in my ears as if they'd been spoken seconds ago.

The vision of me trying to move the ocean was superimposed upon the image of my daily life. The two conversations with my doctors came together with these images like a match and a powder keg. I was astounded by the revelation that finally struck me as truth. I was slowly killing myself (maybe I was quickly killing myself!). The rest of the way home, all I could think about was the absolute necessity of following my doctor's advice of three years ago.

Over the next few weeks, I sought solace in my few quiet moments to contemplate what I should do. Massage kept coming to mind. I talked to my friends about my poor health and my need to have less stress; about the revelations I had had on my vacation; and of the conversations with my doctors. I discussed looking for a less demanding, lower-level job. I brought up the idea of quitting my job and going to massage therapy school.

My friends were in similar circumstances—stress-filled lives that revolved around working too much. They had no answers for me. In fact, they didn't understand the questions, and thought I was crazy for asking them. They wondered how anyone could financially afford to make such changes, and why anyone would consider it. But I knew I could not afford *not* to make a change, so I started searching even more deeply for answers.

When I imagined becoming a massage therapist, even though the idea sounded insane, it was the only time I escaped the strife.

During those moments, I experienced peace, and could clearly see the maelstrom my life had slowly become. I didn't understand why, but this idea felt like the right thing to do.

My logical mind, however, agreed with my friends. It told me this was not a sensible course of action. Going from a CFO to a massage therapist? How crazy was that? Yet, I started researching massage school in spite of the supposed madness of the idea.

After pondering the topic for a few months, I decided to ignore logic. I gave notice at my job, closed out the pension plan I had from my years with WI, and enrolled in massage school. There was no turning back. To be unencumbered by the time school started, I had given an indecently short notice at work, and I refused to share details of my next steps with anyone. To be honest, I felt no one would understand this move, and I didn't want to have to explain or defend it.

I told my kids. Megan was supportive, not knowing what else to be. Jake did not understand and fell into the category of skeptic. "We'll see how long this lasts," he muttered under his breath. Having only spent eight months at the city job probably made me appear reckless in his eyes. The few friends I had told were skeptical, as well. Some thought my plan was hare-brained, though a couple told me I was brave. But I felt no fear and had no second thoughts. It was as if I were in a maze and had tried all the other routes unsuccessfully. This was, quite simply, the only way to go forward.

I started massage school on August 8, 2005, and my soul sang with delight. With the cessation of stress, for the first time in years, I could sleep; I didn't have a headache; I was not in constant pain; and I could suddenly remember such details as how to get to my kids' schools.

Previously, I hadn't fully realized what a toll my job had been taking on my life. Within weeks, two of my autoimmune diseases (asthma and irritable bowel syndrome) vanished. I was able to come off four prescription medications, and I was happy in a way I had forgotten was possible.

I had finally stopped trying to move the ocean, and I was allowing myself to feel the waves flow underneath me, feeling the buoyancy, respecting the power, beginning to understand how to work with the forces to get where I needed to go. A feeling deep inside of me confirmed I was doing what I needed to do to get back to the Path, back to being in unison with the Universe, where I would again have a life of ease.

Massage school was like nothing I'd experienced before. I was in a class of forty-two mostly young people who were excited, impressionable, and eager to get their lives as adults started. I was on the other end of the spectrum, recovering from what felt like a bludgeoning. I was trying to find my way back to the truth I'd known when I was younger; the truth that life could be good, happy, and easy.

School was nine-hour days (broken into two four-hour classes and an hour for lunch), Monday through Thursday. We also had a five-hour student clinic on the weekends, where we were expected to provide five fifty-minute massages to anyone in the public who lined up and paid their twenty-five dollars (which we did not get). The course ran for seven months.

I expected certain classes in massage school: Swedish massage, sports massage, spa treatments. These classes consisted of a half-hour lecture and then a forty-five-minute demonstration, where the teacher performed the skills being taught on a student as we all watched. Next, there was a fifteen-minute break where forty-two students paired off and set up twenty-one massage tables. In the following hour, one student was the client and the second was the therapist, trying to repeat the skillful presentation from the instructor. After an hour, there was another fifteen-minute break, and the students switched roles. Then, we put away the massage tables, and class was over.

I guess I hadn't really thought about what a massage class would be like beforehand, other than the topics covered. What I was most unprepared for was the *nudity!* Depending upon which two classes were taught, a day was comprised of two to four hours where twenty-one people were naked (under a sheet, of course) in one room. When you were the teacher's demonstration student or the client to another student's therapist session, you would climb under the sheet on the table and take off your clothes, tossing them under the table. They would later be retrieved by your partner and handed to you to put back on under the sheet.

If you were the teacher's demonstration student, which I seemed to be an inordinate number of times, you were on the table, naked, in front of the entire class. As I stated before, we did have a sheet on us, but the sheet was removed from the portion of the body being worked, which could be one side of the back (from top of hip to toe), the entire back, or the abdomen (from below the breasts to above the pubis). The fact that the class contained thirty-nine women and only three men (and sometimes a male teacher and teaching assistant) did nothing to lessen my discomfort.

I had grown up self-conscious about everything, especially my body. In school, I wouldn't even shower after PE. I would change clothes as quickly as possible, trying to hide my body the entire thirty seconds in which I had on only my underpants. As an adult, I was one of "those" people who changed clothes in the bathroom stall of the locker room. This part of massage school was quite a challenge for me in the first few weeks. But after a few classes, I was incredibly comfortable with my body and nudity—a side effect that I never expected but very much appreciated.

There were also lecture classes I hadn't expected. Anatomy and physiology, first aid, and pathology were normal academic classes. The teacher gave a three-and-a-half-hour lecture with a few breaks. While most of my classmates had no problem with the massage classes, many hadn't attended college and weren't prepared for real science classes. They had signed up to learn how to rub people, after all. Although I was genuinely surprised at the level of science we were learning, I didn't find it very difficult. Having been a biology major right after high school, then a half-time accounting student and full-time employee, mom, and wife for many years, this was a cinch.

I classified the third group of teachings as "mumbo jumbo" at first. These topics included Eastern-influenced modalities, such as acupressure, reflexology, and shiatsu. We learned about energy meridians, chakras, and auras. I rolled my eyes when my teachers started talking about moving energy and other unusual topics, like the Law of Attraction (manifesting what you desire into your life), using your intuition to treat your client's issues, or even grounding yourself before you went into session.

Then, I started experiencing things I had no conception of before. We learned in reflexology how the areas of the foot mirrored areas of our bodies. By pressing on each spot, we could clear blocked energy in the corresponding body part or organ and help affect healing. *How ridiculous!* I thought.

At the completion of the class, we each had to perform a reflexology protocol on another student. During my turn to receive work, I was miserable with sinus congestion—I was so stuffed-up I could barely breathe through my nose. During the protocol, my sinuses suddenly started emptying and I could breathe freely. I realized the other student had finished working on the area of my foot that corresponded to my sinuses. I wondered if there might be some things in the world I hadn't learned in my data-driven life of the past.

I had several eye-opening experiences like this in various classes, but the most amazing was when I started giving massages. The student clinic was an odd experience—the classrooms had drapes on tracks that were pulled around like an emergency room, making little enclosed areas for massage "rooms."

In the beginning, I was anxious going into the makeshift cubicles. The client would tell me what was bothering them, and everyone in the room could hear my responses. "I have a lot of pain, right here between my shoulder blades."

"That could be from tightness in your pecs, or chest. Do you sit at a computer all day?"

"No, I drive for a living."

"Ah, that is similar, and uses the pecs a lot. I will make sure and stretch those out to see if you can get some relief."

I hoped I said the right things, trying to remember what I had learned in class. I wanted to do a good job, and help my clients feel better. But there were a lot of extraneous issues that plagued me in the beginning.

First, I had to get used to being in a small, enclosed space with a naked stranger who expected me to take away their aches, pains, and stress. I knew what a massage was supposed to do. I'd received many of them and learned lots of techniques in class. But I had not learned every part of the body in the beginning, and I wasn't completely certain what techniques to use for what issues.

Secondly, I had to get comfortable with the feeling of vulnerability. In my old world, being vulnerable meant losing. I never let my guard down or showed any feelings except confidence (even if confidence was the last thing I felt). This person, lying there naked and susceptible, expected me to relate to their humanness and help them. A good massage required vulnerability on the part of both the client and the therapist.

Lastly, I needed to stay in the present moment to generate the intuition necessary for feeling this person's unease, hiding inside their muscles. This was not the kind of work where one should multi-task, which had previously been a way of life for me.

The first several massages I gave were mechanical and nerve-racking (for me, at least). But by the end of my first five-massage clinic shift, I started trusting myself and my intuition about what the body before me needed. I put my hands on my client, and suddenly, I knew what was being called for. More pressure here, less there, and sometimes, I needed to linger in a spot. I didn't know why I was lingering, it simply seemed the right thing to do.

And then I felt it. The energy would move through me. I could feel a tremendous heat come into my body, making me feel as if I were on fire. It went from my hands, into my torso, and out. Then, I sensed a relaxation from my client. They would confirm what I was feeling by telling me, "Oh, yes, that's much better."

This seemed crazy! Not only was I understanding what clients needed with no direct communication from them, but I was feeling the pain move out of their bodies, through mine, and into space. This was way more impressive than the first time I understood how to use a subsidiary accounting ledger!

I realized I was interacting with another human being on an energetic level. It was slowly dawning on me—there were many things to which I had never been exposed, and so much to learn. Massage might be the subject I had signed up to learn, but I was learning far more than what was being taught.

During the seven months of massage school, I remembered how to have fun again. My classmates were young and carefree. On nights when my children were with Scott, I hung out with the other students. We went for fun dinners, had parties, and played games. I felt fresh and alive again, frequently forgetting I was not in my twenties.

I transformed into a different person. I became open-minded, because of my exposure to things that had seemed impossible before. I realized anything was not only possible, many unbelievable things were actually *probable*. Having felt the pain of others through massage, a new-found compassion coursed through my veins. I discovered most people shared my experience of being stuck in a life and body that was killing them. This knowledge shocked and enlightened me.

Halloween brought me an opportunity to see and display the contrast of who I had been and who I was becoming. I dressed up as my former self—facilities division CFO at WI. I wore one of my most flexible business suits and put on makeup (for the first time in months). I brought my briefcase, upon which I stuck a bunch of fake money, spilling out of the pockets.

I received many comments on who I had been only a couple of months before. "Wow! I barely recognized you!" "Oh, I can't even imagine you as a business person." "No, really? You used to be a stuffy old bean counter?" I took it all in and took the comments as supreme compliments about what I had made of myself in such a short time.

The metamorphosis amazed me as well. My life was the simplest it had been since high school. Life now had a plan—a syllabus neatly laid out everything I'd do for the next seven months. I had a set daily schedule—no emergency strategy sessions that kept me for an extra five hours. And I had honest-to-goodness *fun* every day.

On days when my children were staying with me, I hurried home from school and truly spent time with them. I didn't have to check email or finish a last-minute project. I didn't run late because a meeting had expanded past its time limit. I had real energy and was genuinely invested and involved in what they had to say.

One day Megan told me, "Mom, you've changed. Can I give you the personality test again?"

Days before I quit my job, Megan had come home from school with a little personality test. She asked me several questions, graded it, and then pronounced me an "Orange." She showed me on a slip of paper what this meant. I read the description and agreed it was a fair assessment. Now, she administered the test again, and I answered the questions, thinking surely my answers were the same as before.

"Aha!" she said as she finished grading, "you are a Purple!"

She gave me the slip of paper and showed me the descriptions of the old me and the new me. The first results described me using words like ambitious, driven, and demanding. The new description said I was calm, endearing, and compassionate. I'm not certain how scientific this fifth-grade project was, but Megan was certain it was absolute proof of my transformation. It's hard to deny. Orange is definitely different from Purple!

I graduated from massage school on St. Patrick's Day, 2006. My children both came to the simple ceremony. It was very sweet. A few of the teachers made short speeches about going forth and doing good things with what we had learned. Awards were given out. I got two—one for my 4.0 GPA, and the second for getting all "high fives" in student clinic (I was one of the few who had done five fifty-minute massages at every single clinic). I was more emotional about this "trade school certificate" than I had been about receiving my bachelor's degree. And I was prouder of my awards than I had been of my "cum laude" designation on my college diploma.

I started looking for a job right away and was hired quickly. I loved everything about my life. It was magical. I had a job at a wellness center and was trying to create a private practice at my home. I was communing with an entirely different type of people than I had previously known. Through massage, I became interested in many ideas and experiences that were new to me. I started doing yoga, not simply as a physical practice, but to enhance my spirituality. Yoga led me to meditation, which I began doing daily.

The people I now knew drank kombucha, did cleanses, were vegetarians, discussed the Law of Attraction openly and unashamedly, and took classes to enhance their innate psychic abilities. I absorbed it all, becoming infused with the new concepts. There were no debits and credits here, and I savored the idea that many things are real that can never be proven—but can be felt.

One of the amazing experiences I discovered was Reiki, which is "energy work." The practitioner, or energy healer, places their hands on the client—or frequently on their "aura"—and somehow heals them. I made an appointment with Jennifer, who was a Reiki Master. As we began, she asked what I wanted from the session.

"I don't really know. I'm not even sure what Reiki is," I responded.

She explained, we could work on anything—physical, emotional, spiritual—and she would look for energy blockages, or other anomalies. Once these were cleared, I would be free of their influence. "Oh, and you should know, I'm an empath, so I will sense things you might not even know," she added.

Huh, I thought to myself, *I wonder what that means.*

I lay down, and she asked my permission to do the session, ending with a phrase about how it would be for our mutual healing and entertainment. I was amused at the phrasing, and that she felt the need to ask to perform something I was paying to have her do. I consented, closing my eyes and wondering what would happen next.

I wasn't certain if it was simply a product of the music, comfy massage bed, wafting lavender scent, or the Reiki, but I felt completely relaxed. I dropped into a state of deep meditation, which had eluded me in my personal meditation practice. The other-worldliness was worth the price of admission. Thus far, Jennifer had not even touched me physically. After a few minutes, I felt her hand resting on my abdomen, where the front ribs separate. It was there for what seemed like a long time, so I opened my eyes to see what was going on. I was surprised to see both of her hands making billowy shapes in the air above my body. I snapped my eyes shut again, still feeling the pressure that was apparently not a physical touch.

After a while, she finished doing what I assumed was work on my aura. She rocked my head gently to the sides and snuggled her hands under it, supporting my skull. The relaxation became even deeper. I felt heavenly. After a minute or two, she left my head and I felt her hands move along my body. They moved not in a stroking, massage-like motion, but simply lifted off one part and then lightly touched down on another, with a few minutes' pause on each area. For what felt like the next ten minutes, I didn't notice anything more.

Then, there was a sensation of gentle pulling. It was as if tiny strings inside me were carefully being pulled out of my chest. I peeked through a slit under my eyelids and saw Jennifer making a motion near my chest that looked like pulling weeds. She pulled with one hand, starting above my chest and ending the motion several feet above me, and slightly to the side. Then she made a flicking gesture with her fingers, as if she were flicking something sticky into the ether. Next, she repeated the motion with the other hand, and so on. I closed my eyes again, wondering what kind of weeds she was pulling.

Near the end of the session, Jennifer spoke to me quietly. "I need to ask you a question, and I hope it isn't too personal. Is that okay?"

"Of course," I responded, dreamily.

"I am sensing some masculine energy here, in your shoulder. It seems to be from an old lover. Has a former boyfriend contacted you recently?"

Jennifer and I didn't know each other personally. She was usually booked up when we worked together so we hadn't spoken much, other than casual greetings. I was a little stunned and roused from my meditative state, as I replied, "Yes, I've actually had three exes contact me in the last few weeks, wanting to get back together."

"One of them has left a lot of his energy with you. Is it alright with you if I remove it?"

"Yes! Please do!"

I didn't feel anything as she removed this energy and closed our session. She left the room, and I sat up. I felt great!

As I put on my shoes and socks (one doesn't need to get undressed for Reiki), I realized a pain I had been struggling with in my right shoulder was gone. It had been bothering me for the last few weeks, and I had been getting massage, stretching, and taking ibuprofen to get past the pain. It would not ease up. Not until Jennifer removed that masculine energy from it.

Even more amazing than the people I met or the things I learned was how my health had continued to improve. The cure for the asthma and irritable bowel syndrome seemed permanent, as I'd had no problem with either since two weeks after I started massage school. The general aches and pains throughout my body dissipated gradually until they were gone. My severe allergies, which were previously year-round and had sent me to the hospital a couple of times, were about 90 percent better. I still had Hashimoto's thyroiditis, but I was on one-third the medication I had taken a year before.

In addition, I had time to spend with my kids. I took Megan to school and picked her up. I arranged my work schedule on the days I had the kids, so I worked when they were in school. I worked evening and weekend shifts when they were with Scott.

My life seemed miraculous. It was as if I had awakened after a very long nightmare, to find myself safe and sound in a haven. I felt like I was truly living for the first time in many years.

The one disappointing transformation was the disappearance of my CFO salary, and its replacement with the income of a not-too-busy massage therapist. When I'd decided massage therapy could work for me, I had assumed I'd work somewhere while I created my own private practice. Once I got my practice going, I thought I would be making sixty dollars per hour. If I could work thirty hours per week, I could make almost as much as I had made before. But at the wellness center, where I made considerably less than my target, I was not incredibly busy. Although I did lots of marketing for my private practice—chair massage at farmer's markets, massage at sporting events, and proposals to businesses to provide chair massage for their employees—nothing quite seemed to click.

I was supplementing my small income with the money I'd withdrawn from my pension. Whenever I needed a new infusion of money, I'd eye the balance in the retirement account to which I had transferred my pension funds. It was still substantially above the limit I had set on drawing it down. My rough estimate had the money lasting two years, if nothing changed. Then I'd have to figure something out. I prohibited the thoughts from going further. I insulated myself from this potential reality by watching *The Secret* again and following its prescribed steps to successful manifestation.

While I was building my massage practice, I spent a great deal of time waiting for clients. At my job at the wellness center, I had to be on location, and frequently spent three or four hours waiting. I needed something to keep me busy or I would go insane. I decided to write a book even though I didn't really know how to go about writing a book. I'd read plenty of them, so I simply began. (It was not the book you are reading, which was written quite a few years later.)

My subject matter came easily. I frequently gave male friends tips and tricks on how to be a better romantic partner. After I'd give them a few ideas, they'd say, "Wow! You should write a book!" So, I did.

I started by making a list of things I thought I could advise men on and then began writing each of these as chapters. It wasn't difficult, but quite time-consuming—writing and re-writing, and guessing if I was doing what an author is supposed to do. I realized I needed more knowledge to move forward effectively.

One day, a massage therapist at the wellness center mentioned she was going to be working at a writing retreat. Her "other" job (which I discovered almost every massage therapist had) was at the writing center of a university. Through this job, she had met a writing coach. He was hosting a writing retreat and she was coming along as the massage therapist and a participant.

It seemed serendipitous. I had started writing, and almost immediately, here was this opportunity to get the help I needed. I signed up for the retreat and eventually became a client of the writing coach.

My progress on the book accelerated dramatically with Max's tutelage. I completed the book in about nine months and began submitting it to publishers. Sometimes I got rejection letters, and sometimes I got no response at all. It was disconcerting, especially since it felt so synchronistic to have begun writing the book, then stumbled upon a writing coach. This book must be my ticket to *something*, but I did not know to what. I hoped it would be an answer to my ever-shrinking bank balance, but after several months of submissions, I put it aside.

In March of that year, I passed the one-year mark of becoming a massage therapist. It was time to review my progress. Life was still wonderful, except for my financial situation. Unfortunately, it had not occurred to me to change my lifestyle from when I was a CFO to match the budget of a not-too-busy massage therapist. I was still heavily supplementing my income from my retirement account, and about halfway to the limit I had set for myself before I'd have to find a "real" job again.

As I considered my options, my fear-based, logical brain kicked in. It started screeching at me about how it knew I'd fail as a massage therapist, and even though I wasn't at my spending limit yet, I needed to start looking for a job. It told me I would have to go back into financial work. This was the only way. I would probably need months to find someone who would hire a former CFO-turned-massage therapist who wanted to return to financial management.

Then, my calm, soothing, intuitive self stepped in. I had not *failed*. I had become healthy again. I had found something I really loved to do and met people I would never have met otherwise. I had had new and magical experiences. The change in my life had been inspired and was something I was happy to have done. Something marvelous and miraculous could be right around the corner waiting for me. I should give myself—and the Universe— more time, my intuitive self told my logical self.

I bargained with myself, going back and forth like someone with multiple personalities. And I came to a decision. I would give myself five more months of doing massage before I had to start looking for a job. That would be August, and it would have been two years since I quit my old life and started massage school.

Unfortunately, when August rolled around, not much had changed on my financial front. I started looking for a job. I had been too ashamed to talk to any of my friends or family about this decision. I hadn't wanted any advice when I changed into this phase of my life, and I certainly didn't want anyone's opinion about how I was moving to the next. I assumed they, like my logical self, would think I had failed at massage and finally come to my senses.

I did talk to my kids about it. They were not aware of the financial aspect of the last two years. I told them I simply could not afford to do this any longer.

Jake had graduated from high school in May and would be starting college soon. He was busy with plans of his own. He was very supportive and kind, saying this was not a failure, but something I had tried. He was glad I had had the experience.

Megan was sad for me. She understood what massage had meant to me. She had also appreciated, more than her teenager brother who was hardly ever home, the extra time and energy I had for our home life during these last two years.

I decided to apply for jobs carrying a much lower level of responsibility than a CFO, hoping to keep my stress level down. I was keeping some of my massage shifts, because I enjoyed massage so much, and because I was now consulting my budget, which told me I would need the money in addition to the salary of whatever job I would get. According to my plan, I would be able to financially maintain my lifestyle long-term, as well as hopefully maintain my health.

As my screeching logical voice had predicted, it took several months to find someone who didn't balk at my eclectic resume. In December, I got a job as a grant specialist at a university.

Higher education was a different culture than I had worked in previously. They had different rules, which were far less stringent than the ones I had followed and enforced. The fiscal management felt lax. Additionally, everything I did seemed mundane and meaningless. I was bored with the work and the days dragged by torturously slowly. There was no stress, per se, but the tedium was making me restless. I met a few people I really liked and enjoyed. Those friendships, along with doing massage on the side, and having quality time with Megan, kept me from completely losing my mind.

One little complication of Jake going off to college, and me getting
a regular day job, was getting Megan to and from school. She was
thirteen, so driving was three years away. She had changed schools
four times in four years after the divorce, and I had promised her
she would never have to change schools again. Although my house
was in the district where she attended middle school, it was not in
the boundaries of school bus service. In order for her to be able to
get herself to and from school, I bought a small house within her
school's boundaries.

I rented out the house in which we had been living. The old house
was the one I had bought when Scott and I divorced. I loved it and
hoped to sell the new house and move back once Megan either got her
driver's license or graduated from high school. It appeared to be good
timing to buy a house. The housing market had recently taken a little tick
down but was anticipated to go back up soon. It was spring of 2007.

At work, one of the administrative assistants retired. My boss told me there would be a congratulatory lunch at a fancy restaurant downtown, and I was expected to attend. This place was insanely expensive, so my new, financially-constrained self was not looking forward to seeing what my lunch there would cost me.

The lunch was scheduled from 1:00 to 3:00 p.m., so no one would need to go back to work (even though most people did not finish work until 5:00 p.m.). I had some things I needed to finish before leaving for the day, so I got to the party a tad late, at 1:30. There were bottles of wine and appetizers on all the tables. My boss's boss asked me if I'd like a glass of wine, and I said that I hadn't budgeted to pay for wine.

"Oh, no, EF is paying!" she said, as she spilled her glass of red wine all over my best suit.

EF was the enterprise fund, an organization that collected revenue charged to the public when they used the time of university employees. I considered it to be taxpayer money, but it was legally classified as private funds. In my mind, there were thirty people who were supposed to be working, and instead were eating expensive food and drinking alcohol paid for by the state taxpayers. What I saw as a lack of integrity infuriated me.

The next day, I confronted my boss about the inappropriateness of the retirement luncheon. He was completely surprised by my opinion and told me I was being silly. I could deal with being bored, but not with what I considered unethical behavior. I started looking for a job the next day.

I applied and interviewed for job after job for which I was well-qualified. In each instance, the hiring manager seemed to like me, and I felt certain I would get a job offer, but none came. It was maddening, and I felt like there was something else going on, behind the scene—something bigger than the picture I was seeing.

I tapped into something I'd begun to understand while I was doing massage: my intuition. I sensed the Universe telling me there was something I needed to learn, do, or accomplish before I could move on. With this in mind, I concentrated on learning everything I could from my job, which was to help researchers in filling out grant applications for federal funding, then manage the fiscal aspects of the grant. I was the number cruncher and specification-follower behind the curtain for the brilliant scientists who did the research. I made sure the costs were shown accurately, the requirements were addressed, the parameters followed, and the timelines met.

I pored over every aspect of this process. When I got bored during my workday, I searched through the electronic files to investigate how other grant specialists did their work. I studied every page of the grants, even though I wasn't responsible for the grant verbiage. The need to know propelled me to learn everything I could to escape from this purgatory.

At Christmas that year, I visited my family. My stepdad said he needed to discuss something with me before I went home. It was very important. Talking to him was not always comfortable for me. In fact, growing up, if Dad wanted to talk to you, you were probably in a world of trouble. It had always been something to be avoided, so I put him off for as long as possible.

On the last evening of my visit, I couldn't postpone the discussion any longer. He outlined for me a grant he wanted to apply for with the federal Department of Energy. He had the concept for a cold fusion process he swore would change the world. (I can only release this information now because he has passed away and all his records have been destroyed, as this knowledge was very top secret.) He spent several hours outlining how this process would save the environment and make us all rich. He needed to apply for this grant to further his research. Pulling out a huge notebook with the grant notice, he leafed through it, showing me all the paperwork that he must fill out in the application process.

As I looked at the grant application for the Department of Energy, I saw it was *the exact same form* I had been using at work! When he asked me if I thought I could help him, I said, "Dad, doing this has been my job for the last year. Not only can I help you, I know this process like the back of my hand!"

That moment, I started to understand how the Universe works. It was magic. I knew there was something I must do to get out of my current job, but this made it all tangible. It was like someone had shown me the Holy Grail. How had I been oblivious to this all these years? During massage school, I'd watched movies about how a universal energy existed, helping people to manifest the lives of which they dreamed. I'd read books, listened to CDs, talked to friends, and all this information told me that manifestation started with noticing coincidences. I was suddenly certain a universal order existed, and one needed to find the Path in order to use it.

It seemed once you were on the Path, things fell into place as they were supposed to. You followed the signs and your intuition, then you got what you needed to begin the next phase of your life. These theories also said you could manifest anything you needed. You simply had to get clear on what you wanted and move in the direction of your desires. Previously, I had wanted to believe it was true, but deep inside, I was still a little too "practical" to believe completely. This experience, though, created a giant crack in my practical nature. Dad's grant application was simply too amazing to be a coincidence.

Over the next few months, as a third (unpaid) job, I ran the application process for my stepdad. I filled out forms, created indirect cost allocation methodologies, cajoled subcontractors to provide information in the correct format, checked the work and rechecked it. It was *exactly* what I did in my day job, and it was completely clear why I had been stuck there for so long.

Although the purpose of the university job was extremely clear to me, I did not understand the purpose of running the grant process for my stepdad. He did not get the grant, and his process was never tested. He died without seeing his brainchild, which I'm certain was all he claimed it to be, proven. I was a tool the Universe supplied to him, helping him along his Path. I know it was meaningful that I helped him in this way, and it was no coincidence I was prepared for the work required exactly when it was needed. I could only assume there must have been some message the Universe was giving to him, through my help.

Soon after I completed work on my stepdad's grant, I had a breakthrough—I got a job working for WI again, in a different division. I quickly found this division was a fiscal train wreck. There were few internal controls, the administrative branch was dysfunctional, and the rules seemed to change daily.

This division was a conduit for various funding sources. We received contract funding, ran selection processes to choose the best organizations to perform the work, and then passed through most of the funding to pay for the programs. Most of our subcontractors were non-profits.

The division program directors ensured the subcontractors did a good job of running the programs and providing much-needed services. But the financial side of the division was not equipped to oversee the work in a manner consistent with contractual requirements. There was a mixture of fiscal personnel who worked for me, and they ran the gamut from grossly incompetent and taking up space to entirely competent, but beaten down until they could not do their jobs any more.

The organization needed me—someone fresh to the battle, who wasn't afraid to upset the apple cart, and who knew how to manage financial processes. I was the right woman for the job. Unfortunately, division leadership wanted to keep the apple cart as it was and seemed oblivious to possible repercussions from our funding partners.

I realized how difficult the job would be early on, when I found a plethora of issues which needed to be fixed. My alarm increased when I got called into my boss's office to discuss an email I had sent to a subcontractor. They had done something that was flagrantly incorrect. I wrote the president of the subcontractor an email letting her know, in very polite terms, this was a breach of their contract, which guided the reimbursement of their expenditures. I gave a couple of options, showing how the situation could be remedied so they could be paid. I asked her to respond with how she wanted to handle the situation.

I had edited the email at least three times before sending, softening the verbiage with each edit. This was my first interaction with this person, and I wanted to show respect, be considerate, and educate them about the reimbursement process. I copied my boss on the email, so she would be aware of the issue.

My boss was a tough taskmaster and a very direct communicator—two of the many things I liked about her. Therefore, I was quite surprised when she called me into her office and, handing me a print-out of the email, said, "You can't send this kind of email to our subcontractors. This was referred to the division's director, who handed me my ass over it."

"But what did I do wrong? I was very polite and bent over backwards to offer ways in which the situation could be resolved. What was I supposed to do?"

"I know. Normally, I'd think this email was great, but we must handle the subcontractors with kid gloves. You can't communicate so directly. Our executive management will always take their side over ours, so we have to be very cautious."

From that moment on, I felt like I was walking on eggshells. I made changes slowly, enacting one change every six months. Before I announced a change, I would work with my staff to develop a strategy, then present it to my boss. She would generally tone it down a bit, make a few suggestions, then help me meet with the better-run subcontractors to pilot the changes before rolling it out. It was painstakingly slow, and I had persistent nightmares about auditors sending me to jail for conspiring to defraud the funding partners.

But our cautious approach was not rewarded. The subcontractors complained to our director, and the WI Chief Executive Officer. My boss was told to get me to lay low and stop making changes.

Even though I knew the organization was allowing actions that could cost us millions in funding, I was to ignore this information and maintain status quo. This created quite an uncomfortable situation for me.

When I worked at WI's facilities division, we had a very strong fiscal presence. Every regulation, rule, law, requirement, and fiscal standard had been followed to the letter. When I came in and saw all the issues, I thought my corrective actions would make me a hero. But I quickly found myself as the goat.

I was hired for this job only a few months ago, after working at the university for only fourteen months. I didn't want to look like a job-hopper. I toiled at this division for a year before looking for another job. I had no other options. As had occurred at the university, I interviewed for jobs I should have gotten, but did not.

I calmed my frustration by remembering there was a reason I had stayed at the grant job, and there must also be a reason for me to be where I was now. By this time, I had given up doing massage. I was making enough money to get by without the extra income. More importantly, this job required too much of my time for me to do massage on the side. Unfortunately, without massage, there was not much I enjoyed about my work life.

I wondered what I needed to do to get the Universe to let me move on. But my intuition told me I was simply waiting for the right things to happen elsewhere—for the right opportunity to be made available to me. It took another two years for the Universe to arrange itself around my need to exit my current job.

Every day of those two years was a fight. I was fighting with subcontractors who did not want to be held accountable to the rules. I was fighting with my own executive management who didn't want to be the "bad guys" in showing fiduciary responsibility. I was even fighting with several members of my staff, who yearned for the good old days when we didn't do the difficult work of true fiscal management.

I had forgotten how lovely it felt to be in synchronicity with the world, to be doing something soothing and which made me feel good. I careened my way through each day, steeling myself for the stress and dissention I had to endure for eight to ten hours. My mantra had again become, "Anything that doesn't kill me, makes me stronger." I had forgotten about writing, massage therapy, bliss, the Path. All I could do was get the work done before me and hope to find a way to be in less pain—emotionally, psychologically, and physically.

With the decrease in joy and increase in stress, I became aware of my health suffering, again. Everything felt almost, but not quite, as bad as it had been before massage school. My medication for my thyroid disease had doubled from when I was doing massage (but not tripled to the level it had been before that). My allergies were getting worse, and the general achiness in my body was back. I didn't sleep enough and found myself consistently tired. Things were not "as bad" as they had been before, but a nagging worry echoed in my mind.

I didn't discuss my concerns with my doctor, not wanting more dire predictions. Megan had expressed apprehension at my decision to quit doing massage on the side. She knew this meant my life was getting too hectic, but I managed to hide from her and Jake my failing health. She was in high school now and very busy with growing up. Jake had moved back home, but he too kept himself occupied and wasn't home much to notice my tiredness or anxiety.

Finally, it got so bad I decided to investigate what I needed to do to retire at the earliest possible age. I studied the charts of my pension plan and devised a strategy. In leaving my job to become a massage therapist, I had pulled all the money out of my pension plan to support myself. When I started to work for WI again, because I had no account with them, my plan looked at me as if I had never worked toward the pension before. I had started from zero. I would need to attain twenty-five years of service and an age of fifty-five to meet minimum retirement requirements. This would allow me to receive 49 percent of my current pay in retirement. I would need to get credit for as many years as possible, as quickly as possible.

My pension plan allowed me to reinstate the fourteen years of time I had previously worked for WI by "buying back" my time. I'd have to put all the money back that I'd originally taken out, plus a hefty amount of interest.

The first thing I did was pay back the remaining money I'd taken from my pension. I was only able to reinstate, or buy back, three years of service. These three years, added to the years I had been working for WI again, cut the margin down to eighteen more years I'd need in a combination of work and reinstatement. No matter how impossible it seemed, I knew I needed to start somewhere. I would begin to reinstate all the service time available to me—eleven more years. Then, I would only need to work for seven additional years to be able to take early retirement.

I had seven years of working in which to buy back the eleven years of time. I needed to start immediately. I would have to come up with a *considerable* amount of money.

I still didn't see clearly how it could work, as I'd need to pay thousands of dollars a month into my pension over this relatively short time. But my gut told me, if I started, somehow it would all come together. I felt the Universe whispering in my ear. I started by putting $200 per month into my pension reinstatement account. I would never get the amount I needed in seven years with such a meager contribution, but I had to start somewhere.

Interestingly, soon thereafter, my position was examined by human resources. Two similar positions, created after mine, were classified at a higher pay rate. It was determined that my position should be upgraded to match the others, and I received a $300 per month raise. Suddenly, I was putting $500 per month into my retirement plan. Perhaps this plan could work!

I resolved to gradually increase the amount I was putting into my pension account every few months. I would need to be much more frugal than I had been in many years. I started with doing the little things to save, like buying fewer things "out"—coffee, lunch, dinners. I looked for small ways to save money, which I hoped would add up to real money over time.

When I told people about my plan to retire, they thought I was crazy. For me, the decision was for less money and more freedom. It was a decision to invest more in myself and less in my career. It meant seeking health and peace instead of wealth and belongings. Friends asked me, "But how will you survive on 49 percent of your normal pay?" I couldn't answer that question, but I knew, somehow, it would work out. I was headed in the right direction again, and I could feel it.

One day at home, I was sitting at my desk, with a steaming cup of coffee. As I perused my computer screen full of job postings, I wondered what action or revelation would finally get me out of my current job. I clicked on a link, and almost spat my coffee on my computer monitor. Breaking into a cold sweat, I wasn't certain if I was seeing my salvation or my demise. But once again, this was too amazing to be a coincidence. It was the job of budget director for the facilities division of WI, the same division where I'd worked before becoming a massage therapist. This job was a position one level beneath the CFO and was the job I'd had for several years before being promoted to CFO. I was looking at the past, but was I also looking at my future?

I thought briefly about the stress, but quickly reminded myself the budget job was much less stressful than the CFO job, and certainly it would be less stressful than the one I had now. Plus, it would be more money—more input for my retirement plan. "If it doesn't kill me, it makes me stronger," I muttered.

When I thought about applying for this job, I felt a calming sensation come over me. It seemed like what I was *supposed* to do.

When I thought about not applying, I was overtaken with a feeling of impending doom. I remembered what I'd learned when trying to leave the university grant job, when I applied for many jobs but didn't get them. I'd learned I couldn't get out until the Universe was done with me there. There was a clear sign when I could move along.

Perhaps my current job was a holding pattern, waiting for this budget director position to become available. I reasoned that I should apply and if I were not supposed to get the job, I wouldn't. *That's how the Universe works*, I told myself.

I went through the long, drawn-out process. I tested number one on the list of applicants, and I was granted an interview. I left the interview feeling I had done well. Surely, I was the best applicant for the job.

When, in due time, I got the job, I was relieved and excited. This was an organization I had known inside out; where I had basically grown up. I had worked my way through the ranks and it felt like coming home. Of course, coming home isn't always easy, and I would come to find out this job would not be, either.

I hit the ground running. Even though I had been gone for six years, I knew a lot of the people, the issues, and the procedures. Therefore, I could be productive right away. It was a very big, stressful, hectic job, but it was quite nice to be doing things that made sense to me again. It was like I'd walked through hell already, which made everything from there on a relief.

Although the job required a lot of my energy and some amount of overtime, it was manageable at first. Jake was out on his own and Megan had left for college. I was not dating anyone, so I had few demands for my off-work time. I could do my job adequately and still have time to do yoga regularly and have a little social time with friends.

Surely, the Universe was showing me I was moving in the right direction. Getting the same budget director position, which I'd had years ago, seemed like something too significant to not be Divine.

Plus, I felt very happy since I'd come back. The happiness emanated from deep within me. It was certainly a good sign. The Universe was nudging me in the direction of the Path. *I must be exactly where I'm supposed to be, because this is where I am*, was the message I felt in every fiber of my being.

I knew this job was not my Soul's Purpose, but rather a conduit through which I would reach it. Perhaps I had stepped off the Path too soon when I quit massage therapy. Maybe I could have found my Soul's Purpose earlier if I'd stayed the course. Perhaps something had been right around the corner I had never turned because I got the job at the university.

But my intuition said there would be a new opportunity. I felt it would come when I retired. Retirement would be my next chance at doing this right. It was good to be finding a way to retire soon, as I didn't want to put my Soul's Purpose off too long.

As for my retirement plan, I needed to invest in it more heavily to accomplish my goal. I had received another raise with the budget director job and added all my pay increase into the plan, but I needed to do even more. I faced the same problem I had faced when I tried to be a massage therapist. Like most people, I had built a life that required the amount of money I made each month to support it. When I first started buying time in my pension, I had cut out the relatively easy things, and I put my raises aside instead of increasing my spending. Since I didn't want to be in executive management again, I was likely at my top pay rate. There could be no more substantial pay increases, and I still needed to contribute even more.

The house I'd bought when Scott and I got divorced was rented to someone who struggled to pay the rent. Her payments were late and short more often than not. But she had kept her payments up just enough that it wasn't worth the pain and expense of evicting her. Because she was struggling to make the rent payment, I thought it was in both of our interests to get her out of the lease. I hoped she would see it the same way.

We met to discuss the idea, and it thrilled her. She was in a relationship with a man who wanted her to move in with him, but she had told him she couldn't, until her lease was up in eight months. We decided she would move out of my property in two weeks.

I investigated the rental market and found out rates had gone up. I raised the rent by $100 per month and had a new tenant moved in less than a week after the last moved out. I was excited to get my rent payments on time and in full. And I had $100 per month more to put into my plan!

While I was on the housing subject, I looked at my biggest monthly payment, which was the mortgage payments (yes, a first and second) on the house in which I lived. The real estate market was still recovering from the horror of the 2008 financial crisis. Interest rates were going back down. I considered selling the house or refinancing my mortgage, but the market had not come back enough for either to work. I owed $35,000 more on my house than it was worth. No one would refinance my loan, and I couldn't afford to sell. It seemed I was stuck with my largest budget item.

But once I convinced myself there had to be other ways for me to put more money into the plan, ideas started flowing and doors started opening. Within a few weeks of discovering I couldn't refinance my mortgage, I was talking to a friend who had come into a bit of money. She and her husband were trying to figure out the best way to invest it. I wondered if they could loan me the money to pay off my second mortgage. I would give them a full percentage point higher than any fixed-interest rate investment they could find, but it would still be a few percent lower than what I was paying on my second mortgage. If they would loan me the money without putting a lien against my house, I would have some equity and be able to refinance my first mortgage.

I pitched the idea to my friend, believing she and her husband would never take such a risk. But they thought it was a great idea! Within a month, I had the refinance done, and I was paying $300 per month less on my mortgages. I immediately increased the amount I was putting toward my pension plan by $300.

I had gone from putting $200 per month into my pension account, when I had first started, to putting over $1,000. Although I still needed to do more to meet my goal for retirement, I was amazed how well my finances were conforming to the plan. Only two years had passed since I started on what seemed an impossible goal, and I was very satisfied with my progress. I could certainly attain my goal if I kept receiving these kinds of windfalls. I kept looking for signs leading the way and believing things would happen the way in which they were intended.

In the meantime, my job gradually changed. I understood my boss's job well, since I'd had it for several years. When he was having issues with a project, I would try to give him insight. He would say, "It seems like you have a good grasp on this. Why don't you take the project on?" And I did.

Slowly and almost imperceptibly, I took on more responsibilities, more stress, and more pressure. There were more long days and the occasional weekend spent working. During the second year of the budget director job, I started wondering, *If I'm on the Path, why does everything seem difficult? Why is my life becoming painful again? Where have I gone wrong?*

I had felt strongly that I should apply for this position, and I would not get it if it weren't where I was supposed to be. But I had taken on too much responsibility. Perhaps I had veered slightly from the Path. Obviously, I needed to get through this time, and allow the Universe to provide me with the next steps to get back squarely on the Path.

Of course, as my psyche suffered, so did my health. My thyroid medications had to be increased again, back to the highest level they had attained in my previous time as CFO. I was feeling awful most of the time—having even more body-wide pain, mental fog, and exhaustion. My allergies had gotten even worse.

One day, I went for a run. Gone were the days when I ran for the sheer joy of feeling my body move. I was running because it was a nice day, and I was supposed to run on nice days. At the end of the run, my gut hurt a little and my breath was a bit ragged. I thought it was odd as I got in my car to drive back home. My eye felt puffy, so I looked in the rear-view mirror. Uh oh. My right eye was swollen halfway shut, and my face was red. This was anaphylaxis. I knew I needed to get to the hospital. But could I drive? Another look at my face showed my eye was now, only a few seconds later, almost completely closed. I probably should not drive, I acknowledged, and called 911. When the ambulance arrived, the paramedics repeated what others had told me—one does not get this kind of anaphylactic reaction from environmental allergens. "Oh, but you don't know me. I'm an overachiever," I half-joked with them.

I was released from the ER that night, and back at work the next day, with no one the wiser—except Megan, who gave me a ride home from the hospital. I knew my stress at work had caused this increased allergic sensitivity.

At this point in my life, I wasn't surrounded by people who knew a better way. I didn't have time to hang out with my massage friends, or others who believed in a Universe that is filled with magic. And somehow, their very existence had been relegated to a distant memory. I told myself I would have a wonderful life again later, after I got through "this."

The only bright spot was my retirement plan, which was moving right along. When things were at their dimmest, I focused on the plan, and like a flashlight in the dark, it softly illuminated the way. When desperation started to overshadow the flashlight, I questioned if I could accelerate my retirement plan even more.

I searched my budget yet again for something I could give up. At first, I couldn't find anything to create a substantial savings. Then I had an inspiration. With Megan gone to college, I didn't need this house anymore, and the mortgage on it was still my biggest expenditure. I would love to sell it, but it was still not worth enough to pay off my first mortgage and the loan from my friend.

Then I had a ridiculous, amazing idea. What if I rented out this house and moved to a small apartment? I checked out the parameters—what I could rent the house for and what I would pay for an apartment. I leased the house for slightly more than my two loans. I moved to a 619-square foot apartment. I sold almost all my belongings, as they wouldn't fit into my small place and I didn't want to pay to store them.

I even decided not to have cable. It was simply an expense and time waster I didn't need. The only thing I missed from watching cable was football. I joked with a friend about how I'd soon meet a man and move my meager possessions into his huge house. He'd have cable television and NFL Ticket, so I could watch all the football I wanted with him. I hadn't yearned for a man in my life in ages and told myself this was the musing of a stressed-out mind missing its football fix.

These changes created an additional $1,000 per month surplus. I immediately started putting it into my pension reinstatement plan. I was now contributing a little over $2,000, which was amazing. When I started, I would never have believed I would be able to increase my contributions by 900 percent in such a short time. It was still not quite enough to complete my plan, but I trusted things would continue to align themselves so I would be able to retire by age fifty-five.

If work didn't kill me before then. The week after my move to the apartment, it was Hell Week again. The week of meeting with executive leadership had become even more stressful than it had been in the good old days. Before, meetings were stressful because of the sheer amount of work involved. Now, the work was the same, but most of the members of leadership, to whom I presented, were very difficult. My peers and I had a joke that during any given leadership meeting, one staff member would get bellowed at and humiliated in the public meeting. Once one person had received this treatment, the relief in the room was palpable. Although everyone was sorry for the recipient of this month's degradation, we were all equally happy it was over, and it was not us.

This time around, I was the target. In my budget presentation there happened to be a larger than usual number of anomalies. The leadership chairman did not care one iota about the complexity of managing this budget. He was angry because things had not been adequately explained in the packet that was sent out a week before the meeting. He looked at the addendum to his packet, which detailed the additional budget actions. It was bad enough to normally have two or three additional budget requests presented during the meeting, but here we had eight!

I apologized for the last-minute additions. "Each action has an intricate twist, something the project manager didn't realize in time to get the budget request into the earlier packet. When I received these requests, my choices were to add each to the addendum, or completely halt the project. This would not only drastically affect the project end date but could result in owing the contractors larger sums of money."

This did not assuage him in any way. How could staff be so incompetent? How could we not know in advance about these issues?

I tried again. "As I said, there are explanations for each, which you can read in the budget document. The first, for example, is construction of a new facility, which had problems with hazardous materials. The location was not suspected to have hazmat problems, but they dug up a huge area of contamination. It had to be cleaned up immediately to resolve environmental concerns and for the safety of the construction crew. The second one—"

But he seemed to be tired of my excuses and shouted at my boss to get this situation under control. Yet Bill, who simply responded with "Yes, sir," had agreed with my assessment that the last-minute addendums must go through.

When it was over, I thanked the leadership committee for approving all of the budget requests, as presented. With a stiff upper lip, I walked through the seating area, full of interested shareholders; past the area where staff was awaiting their designated time to present; and through the exit, into the hallway, where I could once again breathe. *I will never be treated like this by them again,* I vowed. And I was absolutely correct.

14

With the stress of my work, yoga became my main source of solace. When I walked into the warm, dark studio at 5:45 a.m. every day, my thoughts calmed, and my cares fell away. I got there early so I could sit in the peace after my drive and be completely soothed by the lovely, musky smell of incense. I would lie on my mat, soaking up the relaxation like it was sunshine.

After my fifteen-minute vacation, the teacher would come in and quietly greet us. Turning the music up and switching it to something upbeat, she or he would briefly introduce their theme for the class. This would be some distinctive insight that they had gleaned in the days before the class, from which we could learn. It could be anything from growing and pushing through the pain in an experience, to taking it easy on yourself and not being so serious about everything, including yoga. This theme would then be cleverly worked into every segment of the class.

We would be led in a warm up, and as class progressed, the music would get more vibrant and the yoga more difficult. By mid-class, I was dripping in sweat, my heart pumping and my muscles feeling strong and supple. Next came the gradual descent, when the class started back in the direction of tranquility. And it would end with a few minutes of savasana, or lying on your back and relaxing, with every ounce of worry wrung out like water from a sponge.

It was a one-hour respite from being hassled and harried. I went to yoga class every weekday before work, and at least one day most weekends. It didn't matter how meager the rest of my life had to get to keep funding my retirement plan, unlimited yoga would stay in my budget. It was, frankly, my only connection to sanity.

In October, I got an email from a studio where I did yoga occasionally. The owner, whom I knew, was leading a retreat in Costa Rica in February. The retreat was much less expensive than any I'd seen before, and I could fly on my frequent flyer miles. It sounded like the perfect answer for my stress-filled life! I felt so strongly about my need to do this, I temporarily reduced the amount I was putting in my retirement account to make money available for the retreat. I signed up and put down my deposit right away.

For some reason, this retreat seemed incredibly meaningful in my quest to be back on the Path. Time on the beach and in the rainforest, eating a vegan diet, doing yoga, and cavorting with other yogis—what better way to get back to the Path—or back to rationality? I decided to stay and explore Costa Rica for an additional six days after the week-long retreat. Two whole weeks off work! I would be so relaxed I wouldn't be able to return, I mused.

The intensifying environment at work made the escape even more desirable. We experienced a huge organizational upheaval.

The division, which had previously felt like family and home, now had executive management who seemed to despise all their employees. Most of us were on edge and disgruntled. Many of the highly-respected and knowledgeable managers were either retiring because they could not stand the environment being created or being pushed out for lack of conformity to the new norm.

The increased stress was wearing. I couldn't sleep and was in constant pain. The only thing keeping me going was the thought of how my plan would get me out of this hell in six years.

Those six long years stretched out before me like a prison sentence. It had occurred to me before to accelerate my plan even more, seeking to get out by age fifty. (I was forty-nine.) I needed to get out of this job, before something awful happened to my health. I tried to visualize how it would be possible to quit before the six years were up, but it seemed like an unattainable dream.

I committed myself to the concept. When I went to Costa Rica, I'd take all my ideas and my journal, and I'd somehow figure it all out. I'd meditate on it, dedicate my yoga practices to it, implore the Universe to show me how I could get out of this unhealthy situation. It would all be okay, I told myself. A plan would make itself known during my time away.

In November, I attended a gong bath, or vibrational healing. I had done these before and found them very soothing and full of inspiration. Even though I had decided to refine my retirement plan in Costa Rica, any inspiration I could receive in the meantime would certainly be helpful.

During a vibrational healing, you lie in a dark room (with many other people—enhancing the meditational energy) while a musician plays various instruments—mainly a huge gong, in this instance. The vibrations of the gong and other instruments wash over your body and deepen your meditation.

The purveyor of this vibrational healing brought stones and gems to place on our bodies for use in the healing. I went to look at the items and see what he recommended for me. He asked what I was looking for help with, and I said stress relief and good health. I wasn't happy with my answer but couldn't think of anything else to say. He gave me the stones he suggested for my request, and I walked a short distance away.

I eavesdropped on his conversation with the next woman in line. He asked her what she was looking for, and she said, "Courage." He recommended a heart-shaped stone made of carnelian, a smooth, orange stone. I instantly felt courage was exactly what I needed, too.

I went back and picked out my own heart-shaped carnelian. I used it during the healing and found it very pleasing to hold. It was heavy for its size, and smooth, except for a little crack right across the middle. It fit exactly in the palm of my hand, and when I closed my fingers around it, I felt safe. I placed it over my abdomen during the gong bath, and I swore I felt braver when we finished. I bought it afterwards. Now I had some courage to carry around. Who knew? I might need it.

I couldn't fathom what had happened to me that night, but something had shifted. Soon thereafter, I started experiencing fear on a deeper level than I had ever known. I was panicked almost constantly. I didn't know of what, but I was terrified. I searched for a reason for the fear, but seemingly, nothing had changed. I couldn't comprehend what was creating the terror, which surrounded me. I felt compelled to carry the beautiful orange heart around with me throughout the day. During meetings when I would get anxious, I'd reach in my pocket and grasp it, feeling calmed by its presence. I kept the heart with me constantly. I slept with it on my chest. I had it in my cup holder as I drove. I took it to yoga and put it on the front of my mat.

One day, someone in yoga class asked me the significance of the stone. Without even thinking, I blurted, "It's a symbol for courage, and I have some changes in my life coming up which will require courage."

Oh, wow, where did that answer come from? I wondered. It seemed to come from some wisdom, deep inside me, and the knowledge both startled and enthralled me. As the hair on my arms and back of my neck stood up, my intuition told me soon, I would know what was causing the fear.

I now realized there was a meaning behind my fear, which made it seem prophetic and meaningful, not like some pathetic paranoia or stress getting the best of me. In examining every aspect of my life for the cause, the ideas about my accelerated retirement were a part of the prophecy. However, I could not fit the puzzle pieces together. I seemed to be on the verge of something; what, I did not know, but it must surely be something big. Despite, or perhaps because of, the fear and confusion, I knew I was on the Path and headed in the right direction. I needed to get through this fearfulness and see where I was led.

With all the fear, internal inquiry, and increased workload of getting ready to be away from the office, time awaiting the retreat passed painfully. We were to leave for Costa Rica at midnight on the evening of Presidents' Day (late February), which was a holiday for WI employees. I worked all day in the abandoned office building, trying to get the last details taken care of, as I would be unreachable in Costa Rica. No one, including myself, was used to me being unreachable on vacation, and it meant I needed to have all loose ends tied up. Late in the evening, I left the office with a very strong sense of finality—more so than simply leaving on vacation. I did not know what this feeling meant, but it was freeing.

I scurried home, finished packing, ate dinner, and waited for it to be time to go. Jake dropped me off at the airport a little before ten o'clock in the evening. I went to the gate and slept in one of those extremely uncomfortable chairs. I was exhausted.

I woke about half an hour later to find myself surrounded by my fellow retreat-goers. There was my friend, Katy, the leader of the group and owner of a yoga studio. She would be the main yoga and meditation teacher on the trip and was the only person I already knew. June introduced herself, although we had met electronically. She ran the business end of the retreat and would also be teaching some yoga and art. Next, I met my roommate, Joyce. She was slightly older than I, with an extremely kind smile. She worked as an audiologist. I knew I liked her from the first second I met her. Carrie was a little ball of energy. She reminded me of Betty Rubble on the old cartoon "The Flintstones," with her infectious laugh, dark curly hair, and adorableness. I was surprised to find she was a police officer who wanted to become a massage therapist. There was Stephanie, a voluptuously gorgeous tango dancer, taking a break from her whirlwind travel to settle in with us for a week in Costa Rica. At first, I thought Rhonda and Lisa, who were older women, were a couple, but they turned out to be lifelong friends. Lisa was very quiet, and I didn't get to know much about her. Rhonda was an attorney, whose expression looked like she had just received the most horrible, but not unexpected, news.

There were only two men on the trip. Rob was in his early twenties, about Jake's age, a mathematician and serious recreational athlete—runner, biker, swimmer, yogi. Something about him reminded me of myself, and I believed we had met in a previous life, even though I wasn't certain I believed in previous lives. Mark was a friendly and sweet man about my age, who was a carpenter.

He had only done yoga once before the trip but had signed up because he liked it so much. Also, because he loved Costa Rica.

There were fourteen of us in all. It was a fun group, and I looked forward to getting to know them better. On the plane, the excitement ebbed. I wasn't seated near others from the retreat, so it was easy to settle down, and I slept intermittently. We landed around dawn and gathered together at baggage claim, then took our shuttle bus four hours to Cahuita. By the time we arrived at our beautiful retreat, many of us were good friends already.

We spent a week doing yoga, napping in hammocks, eating vegan food, drinking wine and rum, and doing art projects. A few of us took surfing lessons, went dancing, did improvised moonlight synchronized swimming, or skinny-dipped in the ocean. Except for the yoga, eating, and drinking, I would never have pictured my conservative budget director self doing any of these activities. Because of these fun times, as well as the sense of freedom from being completely cut off from work, it was one of the most life-affirming experiences I've ever had.

For the first time in almost five years, I wasn't Laurie the financial leader who also happened to do yoga and have a small semblance of a personal life. For one week, I was simply Laurie, who was having some great experiences with some great people and learning to live again.

Joyce, my roommate, and I formed an instant and amazing bond. We were in similar places in our careers and had similar fears and challenges. She had been contemplating retirement as well.

"I need to retire soon to save my health," I told her. "I have been developing a plan to retire when I'm fifty-five, but I don't think I can wait that long. I committed to myself to meditate and journal over finding a way to retire next year, when I'm fifty." I admitted I had no idea how I could possibly make it happen, but I hoped something would come to me.

"Oh, I am eligible for retirement now, but afraid to pull the trigger," she told me. She understood exactly what I was saying about health. Her workplace was renowned for the stressful situations there, too.

We discussed the courage it took to make retirement happen for each of us, and the need we both had to bring it to fruition. Joyce's plan came together easily. She had all the pieces and only needed someone to encourage her. I was happy to do so. By the end of the week, she had cultivated a plan.

We talked about my situation, and I meditated and journaled, all to no avail. I was at a loss as to how to make retirement happen sooner than age fifty-five. I felt disappointed with myself at being left out of the inspirational action. I didn't understand it yet, but I had started the ball rolling on my own retirement as soon as I decided I needed to make it happen. The fact I had not planned *how* it would occur was immaterial, or perhaps even beneficial, to the outcome.

On the last full day of the retreat, the yoga class was very impactful to me, in ways I didn't understand at the time. Katy led, having us do the entire class with our eyes closed.

There, in darkness, we could each take the lessons the Universe intended for us. The deepening of my practice brought on by closing my eyes was incredible. I no longer searched the room to see who was doing poses better or who looked cuter in their yoga clothes. My practice was truly about me. I held flying squirrel, a difficult arm balance I had always wanted to do, for the first time ever. I felt each pose as it helped me to expand my body and soul. I had done classes before where the teacher told us to close our eyes for a single pose, and it had been very difficult. This time, I found no difficulty—only liberation.

Katy gives wonderful dharma talks, or themed lessons, during her classes. I was stunned by what she said on this day. Talks during yoga classes stick with yogis because while you're holding the pose, the teacher says a part of the story and stops. Then she moves you through a few more poses, then keeps you in one pose for long enough to say a little more. By the end of the class you have a complete dharma, and the story has had a chance to really sink in. During this class, the dharma talk, which was spoken in short installments throughout the class, went something like this:

The Universe speaks to us in various ways, but we frequently don't hear what it has to say, because we don't pay attention.

The Universe speaks to us in two different manners. At first, it whispers little messages to us. These may be in signs, or coincidences we notice. It may be intuition, or a gut feeling we can't shake. These signs can be easily ignored, because they are small.

Sometimes, these little messages are so subtle we think we are imagining their importance. Perhaps you see an unusual word written in graffiti on a fence, then later in the day, you notice the same word on a billboard. You wonder if this is meaningful, or if you're being silly. The following day, someone uses the word while talking to a stranger next to you on the street. In the evening, you are at the library and see a book with the pesky word in the title. Should you check it out? Absolutely! I think coincidences are always meaningful.

And what if you continue to ignore these messages from the Universe? If it's an important message, the Universe will continue trying to deliver it to you. It will talk to you in the second way the Universe speaks.

If you ignore the whispers, then the Universe will have to yell at you. And you do not want to be yelled at. When the Universe yells at you, the message comes physically. You lose something important to you, or you have an accident, or maybe a health crisis.

The one-word message you kept ignoring in the graffiti and other places was meditation. You think, "How interesting. I keep seeing meditation everywhere. Maybe I should check out that book on meditation and begin a practice. But I don't have time to start meditating now."

You ignored the Universe's whispers, and the next week, you lose your phone. The person who finds it contacts you and you set up a meeting to get back your phone. They ask you to meet them at the school they are attending at night and give you the address. It is a meditation center!

Most of us, by this point, would take the hint and start a meditation practice, but you are way too busy. The next week, you have a heart attack and are in the hospital. Your doctor prescribes therapy—meditation. Wouldn't you wish you had decided to meditate in the first place?

Of all the deep meditations, interesting discussions, and powerful messages that were delivered during the week, this message was indelibly imprinted upon my psyche. It was a palpable moment—as though the message she spoke was for me alone. As if someone took my face in their hands and told me, "Listen to this! It is very important."

After class, we went to lunch, and everyone started talking of their departure, except me and a few other yogis. We were staying on. I was going to hang out with Katy and Carrie for a couple of days until they left, then I was going to spend a few days on my own before returning to home and work. I had enjoyed Katy immensely and found Carrie to be a plentiful source of bubbly, happy energy. I looked forward to spending time with them.

But during lunch, the uneasiness and fear I'd been experiencing before the retreat returned. I hadn't felt it in an entire week, and it came back stronger than ever.

Involuntarily, I began to think I should return home the next day, with the others. I grappled with this feeling for several hours. I told myself I'd be sorry if I left. I thought I'd be angry with myself when I saw Katy's and Carrie's posts on social media about the rest of their trip and how much fun they'd had. I argued with myself incessantly and was angry for even thinking of leaving early. But the fearfulness was relentless. I could think of nothing but my need to get home and decided I would arrange to do so. For the first time since I quit my job to go to massage school, I decided to let my intuition overrule my logical mind.

As soon as I made this decision, the fear subsided, and I was at peace again. It crossed my mind fleetingly—this very moment, when I was making this decision to cut my trip of a lifetime short and go home, was part of the reason for all the fear I'd experienced in the preceding months.

After lunch, back at my room, I got online to figure out my next steps. "Coincidentally," I had purchased my tickets with frequent flyer miles, and there was no charge to change the flight. I was disappointed with my course of action, but the plunge back into fear was only relieved by the decision to go home. I felt at ease and knew this was the right choice, for whatever reason.

That afternoon, I told everyone I would be going back the next day. They expressed surprise and when asked why, I replied, "I'm not sure. It felt like what I needed to do." After Katy's dharma talk about following hunches, no one questioned me further.

On this final evening of the retreat, we had a puja, or ceremony, to close the retreat. We did several ceremonial rituals, one of which was to have one person be the focus, and, going around the circle of yogis, each told the focal person something that had made an impression upon the speaker. During this practice, the bonds between us were cemented. We expressed love, endearment, and wonder to one another.

The person whose comments impacted me the most was Rhonda, the attorney. She told me I had more audacity than anyone she had ever known in her life. It didn't feel like a compliment, although our instructions had been to make all comments positive.

I looked up the word when I got back to my room. "Audacity" can refer to impudence, disrespect, and rudeness, but it also means bold, courageous, and daring. Her words were a forewarning because I would soon need every ounce of my boldness, courageousness, and daring.

The retreat officially ended on Monday evening, with departure around two in the morning on Tuesday. We arrived at the airport around dawn for an early morning flight. I was groggy on the flight, because instead of sleeping for a few hours, some of us decided to enjoy every last moment of the retreat. We spent the final hours visiting, laughing, dancing, and drinking wine until the shuttle departure.

Once home, I slept most of the day Tuesday. When I awoke, I felt calm and composed. It wasn't incredibly bad to have come back when I did. I decided not to let my office know I had returned and do a little staycation. I would relax and enjoy my remaining time off. I felt at peace since I had returned, and I would not beat myself up any more about cutting the trip short. I would enjoy myself and brace for the return to work.

I went to the zoo one day, spent some time reading, and went to a nearby hot springs with one of my few non-work friends. But because I hadn't told anyone from work I was home, I spent the time mostly alone. I didn't get on social media, have lunch with friends, or visit anyone. It was a unique time of introspection for me, and I enjoyed it more than I would have thought possible. It was only four days, and the first three flew by quickly. Day number four would not be nearly as pleasant nor quick to pass.

My last day of reprieve was Friday, as I planned to work Saturday. I decided to take a hot yoga class and get a massage. I went to yoga in a room heated to 110 degrees, for a ninety-minute class. Afterwards, I showered, had a breakfast of celery sticks and peanut butter, and drove across the street to the massage clinic, never suspecting this would be the last time I would drive.

I had a wonderful massage. Every little bit of stress that had begun to build in anticipation of going back to work was released. It was heavenly. When it was over and the therapist had left the room, I stretched and languished in the peace I was feeling. I got up and dressed, then sat down to put on my shoes. I felt amazing!

But when I tried to walk across the room to let the therapist back in, I felt woozy. I sat back down, and the wooziness got worse, becoming a horrendous dizziness.

I was not likely to feel better soon, and I couldn't sit there all day, so I staggered crazily to the door. I opened the door and told the massage therapist I wasn't feeling well. He gave me a bottle of water and helped me back to the chair, saying I could spend some time resting, as he had no clients for the next hour. He left the room.

I drank from the bottle of water and felt worse. Sitting in the chair was terribly uncomfortable, and I slid down to the floor. I still felt horrid, so I lay down with my back on the floor and my legs going up the wall. "Legs up the wall" is a restorative yoga pose that is designed to help one relax and get more blood to the brain.

I had an intuition that told me this was what I needed—more blood going to my brain. But this felt no better, and in fact, I became nauseated. I grabbed some towels off the shelves next to me and began vomiting profusely into them. As I lay on the floor, with my legs propped up against the wall, I filled three towels, even though I'd only had two stalks of celery with peanut butter in the last fifteen hours. I felt like I was vomiting everything I'd ever eaten in my life.

The massage therapist came back to check on me. I told him I couldn't drive myself home and would need to call someone to come get me. He brought my purse to me on the floor, and I called Jake, but got his voicemail. It was the middle of the day on Friday and most folks I knew were at their office jobs, but my ex-husband, Scott, was a real estate broker and he lived in the area. He might be available, so I called him, and he came right over.

I felt like I'd been poisoned, and my body was trying to make everything inside me exit. Scott took one look at me, lying on the floor, puking, belching, grunting, and groaning uncontrollably, and said, "I don't feel comfortable dropping you off by yourself in this condition. You need to see a doctor." He called 911.

When the paramedics arrived, they checked to see if I could speak and control my limbs, which I could. The gurney would not fit through the door, so I was brought a desk chair with wheels, and I wheeled myself to the gurney, as I was still unable to walk effectively. I got on the gurney, and they took me to the ambulance.

As the paramedics were putting me into the ambulance, I looked out through the back door. The world was suddenly a jigsaw puzzle, with some of the pieces in the wrong places. For instance, the female paramedic's face was where her left knee should be. It was a disturbing sight, so I comforted myself by closing my eyes. The paramedics began asking me questions. I understood them perfectly but answering was suddenly difficult. They fired questions at me like bullets. "Can you hear me?" "What day is it?" "How are you feeling now?" "Who is the president of the United States?"

If the answer was more than two words long, I shook my head, "No." Suddenly, it was too much effort to say more than a few words. When they asked questions with short answers, I would decide to answer, but it was excruciating. First, I had to dredge my mind for the correct words. "Yes," became a 100-pound weight that I had to force my brain to lift, then push down to my mouth and coerce through my lips.

After a few moments of short answers that I thought I was managing, the paramedics told me they couldn't understand me. I listened as I tried to ask, "Why not?" and realized everything I said came out, "Mmmuuuu mmmmmuuuuu mmmuuuu."

They began talking amongst themselves, as if I weren't even there. I understood every word they spoke, asking one another's opinion of what was wrong with this woman in their care. One even pulled out a book and started looking up things as they were mentioned—I could hear him flipping pages.

Meanwhile, inside my body that would not cooperate with anything I told it to do (or not do), I finally realized what was happening, and I was silently screaming, "I'M HAVING A FUCKING STROKE!!!!" I became incredibly agitated, wanting to let them know they needed to get me to the hospital, get me the magical medicine that fixes strokes—do *something* you do when people are having a stroke.

Then a thought came to me—the more panicked I got, the more I would hurt myself. I sat back with my eyes closed and began to meditate. *"I'm just surviving this moment,"* was the mantra that came to me instantly. I didn't start the internal chant consciously, but I realized it had started echoing through my mind as I lay on the floor in the massage room. As I repeated it over and over, I knew I would be alright. I had used mantra in meditation sometimes, or when I ran ("One foot in front of the other," got me through a lot of long runs). But it had never occurred to me that a mantra could save my life.

After a few minutes, the paramedics gave up on diagnosing me, stuck an IV in my arm, said they were giving me some meds to stop the nausea and drove me to the hospital. Once at the hospital, it was like a beehive of activity all around me. Scott and Jake were there. People pumped things into my IV, whisked me into rooms for machines to hum and whir and look at my head. *"I'm just surviving this moment,"* was with me every step.

I was in and out of consciousness, with hordes of people talking to me, asking me questions (I could now miraculously speak in a language they understood), wheeling me about, leaving me in the dark, then in the brightness, poking, prodding. And all the while, *I'm just surviving this moment.*

I had times of lucidity when Scott and Jake asked me questions and I answered. I noted Megan was suddenly by my bedside. I wanted her and Jake to know everything was going to be okay. I had no idea if it were true, but I wanted it to be true for them.

Every few minutes, someone from the hospital would come in and ask me to smile, touch my nose, squeeze their fingers, lift my arms, tell them how many fingers I saw, and tell them what day it was. And all the while, *I'm just surviving this moment* was in the background, reassuring me I would, indeed, survive this moment—and the next.

They kept asking me the date, and I knew it was March 1 because that morning, I'd remembered "Rabbit, Rabbit" and texted the phrase to a friend and Megan. ("Rabbit, Rabbit" is a British tradition that suggests if those are the first two words you speak on the first day of the month, the month will bring gifts for you. Boy, what gifts I was receiving!) And I knew it was the same day even though that morning seemed like years ago.

After a few hours, things seemed to settle down slightly. There was no more whizzing into other exam rooms, MRI tubes, or whatever else they had been putting me in. At this point, the doctors began using phrases such as "blockage," and "lack of blood flow to the brain." They told me I had areas of my brain that had become oxygen-deprived.

Somewhere along the way, I became conscious of having only a small window through which I could see. When I thought about it, I remembered it had been like this since I came out of the ambulance and opened my eyes. But there had been so much going on and, somehow, I hadn't noticed it. I saw through both eyes, but only on the left side of each. I called Scott over. "I think maybe I'm blind."

"What do you mean, you think you're blind?"

"Well, I can only see through a little hole like this," I held my hand up in front of the left side of my face, with my fingers joined to my thumb, making a tube.

He called a doctor over, who immediately investigated, holding a finger to the side and moving it across what should've been my field of vision until I reported being able to see it. "It makes sense that you might have some vision problems, as some of the oxygen deprivation was in your visual cortex," he told me, matter-of-factly. Sure enough, I was partially blind. This gave them more to ask me every few minutes when someone checked on me and ran me through my drills.

Various people were in and out, but Jake and Megan stayed as much as allowed, holding my hand, adjusting blankets, looking upon me with fear in their eyes. At one point, I was alone with them both, and I was able to say, "I'm okay. Really, I will be fine. If nothing changes, if nothing gets even a little better, the only difference in my life is I have to take the bus instead of driving from now on. That's not too bad. Don't worry." And to myself, I repeated, *I'm just surviving this moment.*

I don't know when I formulated these ideas, but they burst from my mouth without preparation. My only concern was for my children to not be frightened for me. I had to protect my babies from whatever this monster was that had attacked their mother.

After several more hours of talking with doctors—being poked, prodded, tested, and asked the same questions for the umpteenth time—I was told I would be moved to a different hospital. New paramedics came and loaded me into another ambulance. The apprehension of the last ride started to resurface, but then I remembered, *I'm just surviving this moment,* and peacefulness returned to me.

During the transfer process, my purse, which had been brought with me from the massage clinic to the first hospital, was laid on my lap. I instinctively plunged my hand inside, and there was my orange carnelian heart. I hadn't used it since before the retreat, and it had been forgotten there in my purse. I took it out and held it, enjoying its cool solidity and finally understanding for what I needed courage. *Thank you,* I thought silently.

We arrived at the new hospital and I was poked and prodded for a few more hours, but more gently, less urgently. Around midnight, it seemed to be unanimous—all that could be done for a day had been done. Pain meds (I had a terrible headache) and sleep meds were administered, and everyone disappeared. Poof! I slept. Hard. And still I was comforted by, *I'm just surviving this moment,* not knowing, or caring, what the next moment would bring.

"Laurie, you've had a stroke," said Doctor P. It was Saturday morning, and Jake and Megan had been in my room when I awoke, with the doctor not far behind. I glanced at Jake and Megan to see if the doctor's words were a shock to them. They didn't appear surprised in the least. What we all knew to be my diagnosis was now official. It felt like I'd been waiting weeks for someone to say those words. Now I could move on from there.

Dr. P told me that for most stroke survivors there would be a year of recovery. Because of my great physical condition, however, my recovery period would likely only be about four months. What I heard was that I would have full recovery in four months.

Beneath all the anxiety the stroke had produced, there was a subtle calmness and a sort of knowing. It was as if the stroke was the answer to a question I had not really asked yet. Even in the first hours after it occurred, I was very calm. There was a subtle, underlying assurance, like the stroke was ordained from some higher place.

Once the doctor left, I needed to deal with the real world again. In my real world, I hadn't eaten anything that had stayed in my body for over thirty-six hours. I was ravenous.

I looked at the hospital menu and there weren't many breakfast choices. I told Jake I was ordering scrambled eggs, and he said, "Why don't you have the veggie sausage?"

"Veggie sausage isn't on the menu," I replied.

Then he pointed to the right side of the menu page. When I looked at where he pointed, there were two more columns of choices I hadn't seen before. I would have sworn the menu was blank there.

"Oh, that's weird. I didn't see that column." I added veggie sausage to my order of scrambled eggs.

My food came, and I removed the cover. There, before me, was a round, green plate containing a small mound of scrambled eggs on the left side. No sausage. I turned and reached for the phone, muttering to Jake, "They forgot my sausage."

"You have sausage," was his answer.

"Wow! I see it now."

"Did you miss it in your blind spot?"

"No, I saw the whole plate, and the sausage was not on it. But when I turned my head to the right to get the phone, the sausage appeared from nowhere. The empty plate must have been an optical illusion, I guess."

"Optical illusion of the blind?" Jake chuckled.

"But now, when I turn my head back to where it was before, the sausage doesn't disappear. Like once it was seen, it can't be unseen. What a trip!"

After breakfast, the visitors started arriving. When the first ones, a friend from my yoga class at the gym, Tim, and his girlfriend, arrived, I felt a little nervous. I looked over at the bedside table and saw my carnelian heart. Picking it up, I felt its cool smoothness in my palm, and I was instantly reassured. I put it on the bed, next to me, and it stayed there all day. It gave me the assurance to be positive and hopeful—for my visitors and myself.

I had a stream of visitors all day, with brief breaks between herds, and a minimum of two at a time. I was entertaining—cracking jokes, spreading optimism about my recovery, and making everyone comfortable with me and my plight.

"Oh, yes, my doctor said I'll have a complete recovery within four months. I'll be back at work in two weeks, I bet."

Whenever the recipient of this news said two weeks seemed short, I replied, "I have never missed more than two weeks of work, not for surgery or the birth of a child, or the death of a loved one. Why would a little stroke be different?"

To someone inquiring about me needing assistance because of my visual impairment, I retorted, "Seeing-eye dog? I don't think so, maybe a seeing-eye dude!"

When people told me how good it was to see me, I told them, "It's good to be seen!"

Any momentary break in company was a welcome moment to rest and gear up for the next group. My kids would come over and check me out, asking if I wanted anything. Was I tired? Did I need a break? They helped me out of bed, and got my IV stand over to me, so I could drag it to the restroom quickly before someone else arrived. Standing and walking around were odd at first. I had no physical problems with walking, and thanks to my years of yoga, my balance was perfect. But I had to look around a lot to see where I was going. It wasn't difficult; it was just odd.

I wondered at one point how so many people even knew about the stroke, and where I was. Then I remembered the call from my sister that morning. After getting all the details and being assured I was going to be okay, she asked if she could post something on social media about my stroke. Beth can have a flair for the dramatic, so I reluctantly said yes.

"But don't make it sound awful and do NOT ask people to pray for me!"

I guessed she had made it sound bad enough that many folks thought it important to take a few hours of their Saturday to come check it out. And I'm certain some of them did pray for me anyway.

Around dinner time, the visitors cleared out and it was only me, Jake, and Megan. I stopped entertaining and started noticing things again.

It had happened without me realizing it, but by the end of the day Saturday, there didn't seem to be any blind spot. I could see everything in my hospital room. The entire room was laid out before me. I thought I was cured. The only hint of a problem was the frustration when I tried to read anything or look at something small right before my eyes. In addition, I could only see half of people's faces. I managed to ignore the disconnects and, without even thinking about it, believed these anomalies would soon go away.

When people had given me cards, I hadn't opened them. I simply put them aside and said, "I'll read this later." (I read them six months later.) When I was forced to look closely at something, like the menu for my meals, I had to face the small window of vision I possessed. But the rest of the time, I could be comfortable in my belief I was cured.

I spent all of Saturday basking in this illusion. I kept myself busy entertaining my friends who visited and being positive. It was a nice day of make believe.

Sunday morning, Jake called around eight o'clock to see how I was and ask if I wanted him to come to the hospital. He'd been there with me until midnight on Friday, and most of the day Saturday. I told him to relax a bit and come later, when they'd be releasing me. I would need a ride home—because my car was still at the massage place.

For the first time, I was awake and alone with my condition. I didn't understand the difference between how I was able to see the whole room but could not read a simple menu. Only last week, I was in a land where I didn't understand the language I heard spoken, and now I was in a land where I didn't understand what I saw— where people only had halves of faces and sausages hid in plain sight. I didn't understand how this had happened to me. I suddenly felt small and alone, and scared. It shocked me when I admitted to myself I was scared. Hiding from the fear meant occupying my mind with other thoughts, so I tried to keep myself occupied.

Jake had taken my clothes home because I'd thrown up on them. Megan had packed me some comfy yoga clothes for my departure, but I had no shoes. My thoughts ran in circles around my head like children playing tag. *Crap, how can I go home with no shoes? How can I even have no shoes? I have some people who volunteered to bring me food this week. Who's bringing what when? And I'm supposed to make appointments with my doctor and a neurologist. When will they be? How will I get there? Details. I can't grasp them all. I need help. I need my Mommy. I'm forty-nine years old and I need my Mommy.*

I got my phone and found her on it, and I called. "Mommy, I need your help. I don't have any shoes and I don't know who is bringing dinner when, and I need someone to take me to the doctor. I need you, Mommy." That's not exactly what I said, but it's what I meant. I'm sure I said something that sounded much less helpless and much more self-sufficient. After all, I was Ms. Self-Sufficiency.

Mom said she couldn't come during the current week. She needed to take care of my stepdad, who had recently had back surgery, and she offered a few other excuses. None of it rang true. I sensed something from her. I sensed she was scared, too.

I guessed she must be terrified of what she would find, and this thought helped me to be brave again, if only for a few moments. I soothed her. "Mom, it's okay. I'm really fine. I don't look scary, and I can do everything I did before, except I don't see very well. It's okay, Mom, don't be frightened. I really need someone to help me get to appointments and keep track of things." She assured me she would work something out. She would get me help until she could get there.

I hung up the phone and I was alone again. And scared again. It's easy to be brave for your children; it's easy to be brave for your friends; for your mom and sister; even for your nurse. Being brave for yourself, when you're the only one in the room, the only one showing up—*that* is difficult. Sooner or later, you must admit to yourself the bravado is false. And when there are no distractions or fanfare or people for whom to be brave, you cry. And that is exactly what I did. I cried hard for about two hours.

When I'd run out of tears, I convinced myself I was going to be okay, and I stopped crying. Then came the pain. Having a stroke gives you one hell of a headache. When you cry, something happens, creating another headache. Put the two together, and they won't give you enough oxycodone to cut the pain.

Jake arrived and knew what to do. He put a cool, wet cloth over my eyes for me, held my hand, and simply let me be, exactly like my mom did when I was a little girl. Exactly like I did when he was a little boy. I could allow the troubles to fall onto his big, broad shoulders for a bit, and I slept. I slept with fear and hope and doubt and the assurance of knowing Jake was there, holding my hand.

Before it was time to go, Jake suggested I might want to take a shower. The thought hadn't occurred to me, but it sounded wonderful. I felt fine, except for the horrendous headache that was exacerbated by any quick movements. Since Friday night, the IV stand had been my constant companion, going to the bathroom with me. They had removed the IV, and it was freeing to be able to move about for the first time without it. After the shower and getting into my own clothes, I felt more normal. And, miraculously, I had shoes, which Jake had brought me.

I was ready to be released from the hospital. They took me to a conference room down the hall to go over paperwork. Jake continued his parental role by reading the paperwork for me and helping me find where to sign. I didn't have to ask, he simply told me what items said, and pointed to lines requiring my signature.

As I left, I tried not to notice it was scary going down the hospital hallway. It was so wide-open, and I had to move my head from side to side to see the breadth of it. It made me feel small to be in a wide-open world. I couldn't take it all in visually without great effort. When I got into the car, I didn't focus on anything. I felt lucky to have the sun shining through the windshield on my upturned face, to be alive, loved, and cared for. And not alone.

My sister, Beth, had arranged for my aunt to come on Monday and stay with me until my mom came the following week. Without my input, it was decided I would stay with my friend, Tracy, and her husband, David, overnight. I objected, saying I was an adult and could stay at my own home alone for one night, and everyone except me knew the objections were ridiculous.

Tracy and I had worked together at WI and known each other for over ten years. She knew when to let me live in my imaginary world of okay-ness, and when to caution me. As we visited, I would occasionally say something—such as predicting when I'd be back to work—which prompted her to exchange knowing glances with David. Then she would say, in a soothing voice, "Well, maybe you should wait a little while before you make any decisions."

Monday morning, Tracy made me a beautiful breakfast of eggs and fruit and a bagel. I felt like a princess being served in their gorgeous home. They had to leave for a meeting, and I was left alone. I laid on the couch with the television on and rested.

It was nice, except watching television was uncomfortable. I couldn't really see what was on the screen, so I used it as background noise to my drowsy reverie. I still couldn't put the pieces together as to why I could see some things relatively easily and others were difficult, and I still didn't want to think about it.

When Tracy and David returned from their meeting, it was almost time for me to leave. David gathered up the small bag of things I had in the guest bedroom and brought it downstairs to me. Tracy fussed over me, asking if I needed anything to eat or drink. I did not. Jake arrived, and I was handed off to him. As I was leaving, Tracy gave me a big hug and whispered, "I love you."

"I love you, too. Thank you for everything." I don't think she noticed the tears I blinked away as we ended our embrace.

A quick hug from David, with an admonishment to take care of myself, and Jake and I were on our way to my apartment. My Aunt Sherry was flying in from Texas, then Beth had it lined up: after Mom came the following week, it would be Megan's spring break and she could take care of me. Then Beth would come. We'd see what happened afterwards. An entire month was covered. I had no idea what to expect in five minutes, much less four weeks. I had to admit it felt good to have someone to rely upon, someone who was assigned to me.

With Aunt Sherry coming in the late afternoon, I had my first post-stroke transportation challenge. I needed to get her from the airport to my apartment. At first, I wasn't sure how to proceed with asking for help. Megan was back at school, and Jake needed to catch up on work after committing most of his time since Friday to me. I was timid about calling friends and asking them to help me. This was partly because getting repeated *No*s would be time- and energy-consuming, but mostly because I didn't want to feel rejected. Social media was barely beginning to get traction with me at the time, so it didn't instantly occur to me to use it. But when I peeked at my account, I had dozens of notifications. Tons of people had "liked" the post Beth had made about the stroke, and many had responded by offering help. I posted a plea for help, asking for someone to pick up my aunt from the airport.

Within a few minutes, it was arranged that a friend from high school, who had moved to Colorado, would help out. I was amazed it had been so easy to ask for, and receive, help.

In the afternoon, Lettie brought my aunt to my apartment. After she left, Aunt Sherry and I went over the standard first-conversation-after-the stroke discussion—a detailed explanation of what happened on the day of the stroke, followed by information on the effects of the stroke, my capabilities versus disabilities, and current prognosis. I had practiced many times in the hospital, and I had the patter down.

Then Aunt Sherry prepared dinner from the groceries I had. I soon needed to retire to my bedroom and she was left to amuse herself and sleep on my couch. I felt badly that she wouldn't sleep in my room, but she insisted, saying someone who had had a stroke four days ago should not sleep on the couch.

The next day was a blur. Aunt Sherry took me to my primary care physician. She drove my Honda, which Jake had retrieved from the massage clinic and placed in my garage. At the appointment, my doctor told me I could walk and do yoga, but I couldn't put my head below my heart. Fifty percent of yoga class has the head below the heart. I argued with her about this until she got blunt with me. "Look," she said, "this is your brain we are talking about. It has received a grave injury and needs time to heal. If you don't take the proper measures to allow healing over the next three months, your life will be severely impacted."

I had never actually followed any doctor's orders before. When I had my babies and a hysterectomy, I was told I needed six weeks off from work to rest and recover. In all three instances, I was working from home on the computer as soon as I could sit up, and was back at work, at least part-time, within two weeks.

But my doctor's earnestness and the severity of her words told me I must pay attention and follow orders this time. For the first time, the critical nature of my situation hit me, and I surrendered to the idea that this was serious, and I needed to do as I was told.

After the appointment, I was more somber, but still managed a cautious optimism about getting back to work and being back to normal soon. We went home, and I needed to rest. After my nap, Aunt Sherry reminded me what my doctor had said about physical activity. Walking and being physical were good for me. We went for a walk, and although it still felt odd to be out in wide open spaces at first, I felt much better afterwards.

In the evening, someone brought dinner and visited with us. I continued to be entertaining and optimistic, and I added, "And I can't put my head lower than my heart," to the first-conversation-after-the stroke discussion. Our company left soon after dinner, and again I went to bed and left my aunt to her own devices.

I had now been back in my little apartment for a few days, looking around at familiar surroundings and becoming comfortable with my post-stroke vision of it. In creating my new home, I had made a little Shangri-La for myself. Tracy had helped me with the design. There was a beautiful Buddha painting, with orange and turquoise hues surrounding the young, slender Buddha. The rich, mahogany tables and the entertainment center were of Asian inspiration, and an exact match for the armoire Tracy had found on Craigslist for next to nothing. The crowning (or flooring) glory of the room was the opulent and plush Oriental rug that featured the same vibrant colors as the painting.

The tiny dining area had been transformed into a meditation palace, sectioned off from the rest of the room by a dark, wooden Oriental screen, which enclosed my meditation altar.

My bedroom was simple, with my queen mattress and box spring on the floor. I'd sold the sleigh bed and dresser before moving to the smaller living space. I had a light-green and brown comforter. It looked beautiful with the lovely rug I'd found in Fort Collins on a visit to see Megan at college.

As I took it all in, I felt pleased with how elegant and simple it was, and I thought I could see everything perfectly well. I fell into thinking I was cured (again).

I had an appointment with a neurologist Wednesday, and she was going to say I could drive next week and return to work whenever I felt like it. Everything was great. My only limitation would be keeping my head above my heart for three months. I had to acknowledge reading was difficult, but that would clear up, I told myself. I ignored the times when I was looking for something and couldn't see it on the table right in front of me. Then I would move my hand across the tabletop and touch what I was looking for or move my head just right and it suddenly appeared. I didn't think about how dark the world had become, or how I still couldn't see the right side of anyone's face. These were simply technicalities that would improve with time.

Mid-morning on Wednesday, my aunt and I left to drive to the neurologist's office. When we got in the car, it was difficult for me to see anything. Unlike moments ago, in the apartment, my vision was a small space right in front of the left side of my face. I was suddenly terrified, as if this were a new phenomenon.

"Where are we going, Missy?" my aunt asked, cheerfully.

"I…I don't know. I haven't been there before. Here's the

address," I said, and handed her a piece of paper with the office information on it.

"Ok, I'll look it up on my phone."

I stared at the floor to avoid the uneasiness of not being able to see correctly, as she eased my Honda out of the garage and began our GPS-guided journey to downtown Denver.

I instantly connected with my neurologist. She wore an Asian smock and had a very calming demeanor. She seemed to understand me and could tell I knew a lot about the body, especially mine. She also seemed to detect I was a direct communicator, who preferred realistic information. She didn't sugarcoat anything.

We talked a few moments about what I'd experienced during the stroke. She did the test where she started her fingers in my blind spot and moved them toward the front of my face until I announced I could see them. Then she said I had a very large field cut in my vision caused by injury to the visual cortex of my brain.

"The visual cortex," she explained, "is set by age six. It does not change, regenerate, or heal after this age, unlike other areas of the brain. There will not be improvement in your actual vision beyond what you have now. This is as good as it gets for you."

I swallowed hard and barely kept myself from whispering an obscenity at her pronouncement. I remembered the neurologist at the hospital, who had told me my healing would be complete in four months. I had decided he meant I would be completely recovered in four months, but now I understood I was mistaken. I would simply be as healed as I was going to be, by the end of four months.

My neurologist broke my flashback by instructing me to perform some balance tests, and she was amazed at how well I did. The stroke had originated in my cerebellum, where balance is maintained. In addition, visual problems usually entail adjustment before balance can return to normal. Mine was better than people who had not had a stroke or visual impairment, she noted. "It's all the yoga I do," I said, remembering doing flying squirrel pose with my eyes closed in Costa Rica, a mere nine days ago.

She ended the appointment by agreeing with my doctor about the head above the heart situation and added the most interesting and depressing prognosis of all. "You should never drive again."

"What? *Never*?!"

"Never. Patients who have the condition you have kill so many people every year. You are blind in the space where your brain interprets the signal from the right side of both eyes. There is nothing wrong with your eyes, so the signal goes to your brain, but the damage keeps it from understanding the message. Because the brain hates a vacuum, yours wants to fill in the space where it has no message. It simply makes up what it thinks belongs there and paints it over the blind spot. If you were to drive again, you might see a wide-open road, but there could be a car or a pedestrian crossing the street in your blind spot. You would run right into them, never knowing what happened until it was too late."

I thought I had mentally prepared myself for anything, but it was an emotional kick in the gut. The incidents with the hospital menu and the sausage suddenly made sense, though.

Aunt Sherry took me home, and again I stared at the floor. But this time, I stared not because I was trying to hide from my condition. This time, it was because I was in shock at my condition. Aunt Sherry must have sensed my need to be quiet, because barely a word was spoken on the twenty-minute ride.

At home, I used the restroom, and noticed the quote on my mirror, which I had written before I left for Costa Rica. I hadn't noticed it in the days since returning from the hospital, but now it glared at me, knowingly:

"We must be willing to let go of the life we have planned, so as to accept the one that is waiting for us."

--Joseph Campbell

I tried to remember the great dreams I had had for the life that would be waiting for me if I only let go of the life I had planned. I hadn't exactly let go, but instead had my old life wrenched from my hands, like a rope being pulled through my clenched fists. It left damaged palms and hopes of healing correctly, but I knew the scarring was permanent. And what of the life waiting for me? How could it possibly be worth what I had given up? Whatever came next was most definitely not what I had had in mind when I wrote this quote on my mirror a few weeks before.

In the spirit of trusting what was coming next, I began to actively observe how my brain worked. I now understood the difference between being able to "see" my entire apartment and not seeing a pen sitting on the table in front of me.

When I was somewhere I had not been since the stroke, I would "see" my blind spot. It was the same sensation as being blinded by the sunlight. An entire part of my vision was blacked out, and that black spot followed my eyes. When you're blinded by the sun it slowly fades as your eyes recover from the blast of light. For me, the black spot faded much more slowly. It faded because my eyes darted around the room and gathered information. I never decided to do this; my brain, somehow, knew to tell my eyes to do it. This visual information was used to populate a database, which my brain accessed to show me the scene. The database didn't have to be complete for my brain to create the image. It simply needed some ideas of what the area looked like, so it could guess the rest and, as my doctor said, paint over whatever was actually there.

I once saw a dog, with his leash standing out straight from his collar, but no one attached to it, then a woman suddenly appeared from nowhere, holding the leash. Another time, I saw a woman walking along, talking to nothingness. (This was before Bluetooth earpieces made this a common occurrence.) As I tried to figure out if she was talking to herself, her companion passed from my blind spot and appeared from thin air, a few feet in front of me. She looked at me awkwardly, and I realized I was walking straight toward her, not moving to make space. I could imagine this happening with an entire car, as my neurologist had warned.

When the view was of something quite simple, like the top of a table, my eyes didn't even search, and my brain did not question. The picture was spontaneously generated, and it covered whatever I had not seen with what it decided belonged there, like the invisible sausage covered by the vision of the plate in the hospital. Sometimes I saw a tabletop with nothing on it, but I knew I had moments ago laid a pen down there.

I began finding it easier to not use my eyes when looking for something. I stopped turning on lights. I stopped allowing my eyes to focus on surfaces where I was trying to find things. Instead, I felt around with my hands. I discovered—the hard way—I should figure out if a piece of bread was moldy by smelling it, rather than looking at it.

These experiences with my vision were teaching me to suspend disbelief. I looked at a table and saw nothing on its surface. In the past, I would not have believed there was anything on the table, but I had learned to investigate further. I learned "no" actually meant "maybe." "There's nothing to see here," became, "Investigate further. Anything is possible."

This lesson of suspending disbelief expanded to other areas of life, unrelated to my vision. I had believed a lot of things about how my life would unfold. If I had previously been told I would have a stroke and be calmly assessing my deficits and evaluating how to move forward with such composure, I would have thought it impossible. This suspension of disbelief allowed me to postpone my judgment about what the stroke meant to my future, allowing events to unfold as the Universe intended. Even when I was upset or panicked, there was a calmness underlying everything, which said, "This might be an opportunity instead of a condemnation." I simply needed to remember to listen.

20

Aunt Sherry was supposed to stay until Tuesday, when my Mom would arrive, but I wanted to have a few days of exploring life on my own. She had flown on a friend's buddy pass, so it was easy to change her flight to Friday. As she prepared to depart, I thought about how much my aunt meant to me. Aunt Sherry had always been very special when I was a little girl. She had two sons and relished the girliness fix she got from spending time with me and Beth. When my mom was struggling financially, she and her ex-husband were our Santa Claus, secretly giving us a swing set and tricycles. She treated me like a "young lady" instead of a little girl. I felt grown up and very loved in her presence. We had drifted apart as I grew up and moved to Colorado. This time together, with her being my first in-home caregiver, had created a new bond. I was truly sad to see her go and looked forward to getting together again under better circumstances.

Tracy worked at the airport, so I arranged Aunt Sherry's ride with her. She showed up, checked in on me, gave me a hug and admonished me to take care of myself. Aunt Sherry enveloped me in a long, protective, loving hug. "I'll be in touch, sweetie. Take very good care of yourself, and don't be afraid to ask for help. I love you very much."

"I love you, too. Safe travels." And instantly, I was alone. Alone with my thoughts and my new life, for four whole days.

One week had passed since my stroke, and it felt good to be independent. I cleaned the apartment and did a lot of soul-searching and thinking, which I had been avoiding during the last week. *How do I fit my old life into my new life with this disability? What is my disability? How do I deal with the visual and cognitive impairment? And how the hell did words such as "impairment" and "disability" ever come to describe me?* I decided these questions, which were bombarding me, should be put aside until the Universe showed me the answers.

Aunt Sherry had seen the puzzling I was going through, as well as the enlightenment which was occurring for me. After my neurologist appointment, she recommended journaling about my navigations of these experiences. She thought it might be an interesting article or book someday. I immediately started writing in an electronic journal every day. In addition to creating a record of what happened, the routine helped me sort through some ideas and remain calm while I awaited the outcome of this voyage I was on.

The weekend alone passed quite quickly, and soon Tuesday arrived and Mom was due in the evening. I had various activities to keep me busy all day, and then I sat in anticipation of her arrival. All my life, my mom had been a nurse and a teacher to me. When I was sick, I tended to run extraordinarily high fevers (104+ Fahrenheit). She was always there with the Dr. Pepper and crackers. She placed the cool rag on my brow, and the kiss on my forehead that accurately gauged the presence or absence of a fever. She understood, even when the diagnosis wasn't about physical health, it didn't mean there wasn't nursing to be done. Sometimes the illness was in the heart, and she always knew precisely how to hold me and stroke my hair and instill the knowledge, "Everything's going to be okay." And it always was.

I learned the most important life lessons from her. She taught me to act like a lady and think like a man, and that I could do anything I put my mind to. I learned from her "Pretty is as pretty does," which meant being the kind of person people love, regardless of my appearance and abilities. She taught me that sometimes, bad things happen to good people, and that's a shame. But I must carry on, and I could be much stronger than I ever thought I could be. I learned "Life isn't fair, and the sooner you learn it, the better off you'll be," and more importantly, how to live with that fact. She taught me to be happy with what life gave me, and how to get life to give me what I needed. And I learned no one will ever love you unconditionally like your mother. As I thought these thoughts about my mom, I knew she had prepared me for this part of my life, and I was so happy to have her with me.

Scott had offered to give her a ride from the airport. When they arrived, he stopped in briefly to see how I was doing. Mom pulled me into a big, momma-bear hug, and whispered, "I'm so glad you are okay. I love you so much."

"I love you, too, Momma," I answered, a little teary-eyed.

She did the usual, mom things—she made sure I was comfortable, offered to make me food, to take me to the store. She offered her love and her support, asking questions to draw me into talking about the stroke. She needed to know how I was affected, and what I foresaw for my future. I talked to her honestly about the stroke, but only about the logistics, not about how I felt about them. I told her what my doctors had said to me. I told her, as I had begun telling my visitors and friends, the doctors had said I would never really recover from the damage the stroke had done. I gave her lots of information, so she didn't even realize I wasn't telling her anything about *me*.

After thinking all those tender memories about what an amazing mother she had been, I was still not able to allow her the opportunity to nurse and teach me more. During our week together, I never let myself be vulnerable or needy in her presence. I never let her know I was scared or how much I needed to be nurtured.

We had a nice, normal visit. Most of the time, a fly on the wall would have had a difficult time discerning I was having a hard time understanding the changes to my life, was a little scared, and needed my Mommy.

All too quickly, the time for her visit was over. As she was preparing to leave, she began fussing over me in a way she hadn't since the first day. "Are you going to be okay by yourself?" as she fluffed the pillow behind my back. "I bought some groceries, but can you get to the store?" as she brought me a cup of coffee. "Do you have people to help you?" as she kissed my forehead, unconsciously checking for a fever that had no reason to be there.

"Yes, Momma, everything is going to be okay," I echoed her words from so many years ago. And then, I realized I wasn't the only one who had been pretending all was normal. She and I had both been hiding our fear and concern, putting forward a brave face, to protect the other from her own fear.

Jake popped in to pick her up, and I realized I hadn't heard from him all week. He had been at my side almost non-stop for the first three days after the stroke. Then he had come by a few times during the weekend between my caregiver shifts with my aunt and mom.

At the beginning of Aunt Sherry's visit, then again at the beginning of Mom's, he had sent me a text to make sure everything was going smoothly. Then, he had left me to their care and taken care of himself and his life. I wondered if he, too, had been pretending nothing had happened and that he wasn't scared. I guessed he had also been steeling himself for when I had no caregivers and he was my primary help.

His greeting hug held the answer to all my curiosities. Jake is the best hugger of all time. He creates a huge sense of love inside himself, then really, honestly hugs you. You feel the love flow from his heart, which is so near yours; the sweet encircling of his arms around you; and the compassionate pressure of his hands against your back. He has admitted that, sometimes, he intentionally holds a hug until the recipient squirms a little. Then, he intensifies the hug a bit and releases his huggee, who now feels fully and totally loved. This was exactly the hug I got, times one thousand.

Mom gave me a nervous hug, a kiss on the cheek, and said, "I love you very much. You'd *better* take good care of yourself," in the motherly tone that means, *Or else!*

With her departure, Mom took with her the bravado I'd used to ignore the ways in which my life had changed. With no further need for a façade, I could acknowledge, to myself only, I had been hiding the truth from both of us. This hiding was different, though, from the hiding I had done the first week after the stroke. The original hiding had been a complete denial of reality; a failure to comprehend the truth of the situation; an inability to grasp the facts.

This newer hiding was a sweeping under the carpet of what had been discovered. It was, partly, an act of courage that kept my mom from understanding what I was starting to know—I would never be the same. But it wasn't simply hiding facts from Mom that kept me pushing the fear and truth away. There was also an underlying sense telling me, in fact, I *would* be fine in time. It was okay to ignore this fear, because it was based on old assumptions of what life should be. Now, I would look for a middle ground— the plane between pretending I was going to be "back to normal" and pretending my new normal was not an adjustment at all. And that plane was full realization that this, indeed, was my life, and it was good.

I cancelled the remaining chain of caregivers Beth had set up, preferring to start my new life right away. I needed some time when there was no one on the other side of the door giving me a reason to get out of bed and act brave. I was a little tired of it all and wanted to stop telling the stories and explaining my condition and dealing with other people's feelings, expectations, and beliefs. It was time to start developing my own feelings and expectations and learning what my new life would be.

Figuring out what my new life would be involved finding how it fit with my old life. Getting back to work at the office seemed to be the first step. I didn't know how to approach the decision. Physically, I felt normal, except for the need to sleep a *lot*. I guessed I would need to go back part-time, at first, and work up to full-time.

I knew I wasn't ready as I hadn't even taken a bus and had no idea how to use the transit system. And I didn't really understand how working might affect me. Like throwing a dart at a dart board, I grasped at two more weeks as my imaginary deadline.

I called my boss and got his assistant, Trish. We knew each other well because I had hired her as my assistant when I was the CFO. I told her I needed to talk to Bill about when I would return to work.

"Oh, I got the FML paperwork from your doctor last week," she replied.

My doctor had filled out the Family Medical Leave forms, which must be done when one has a "serious medical condition." This legally required document tells the employer what type of restrictions the employee has, and when they can go back to work. It is non-negotiable by employee and employer. What the doctor says is what must happen.

I had received this very paperwork several times as a supervisor of someone who was seriously ill. I had completely forgotten about how it would apply to me as the patient. In addition, it had not occurred to me the doctor would send in the paperwork without a discussion between us.

"It's weird she didn't send it to me. Well, I was thinking I'd return to work in a couple of weeks," I said.

"You can't. Your doctor said you have to be off until June 1, then come back part-time."

I was shocked and speechless at this revelation. After a few seconds to gather my wits, I said, "What?! Three months? How ridiculous! I can't be away from work for three months."

"There's no choice. Doctor's orders." I could hear the smirk in her voice. She was the one who had wanted to call an ambulance the day I was having chest pains. She knew I would overdo it, if not for the pieces of paper she held.

I said good-bye through a stunned fog and hung up. I immediately emailed my neurologist. I told her I needed to go back to work sooner than June 1. I had a lot of work to do and would be out of sick leave at the end of March.

I received her return email much quicker than I had anticipated— within a few hours. Her answer was the same as that of my primary care doctor, when I had questioned the head below the heart limitation. "Your brain must have ample time to heal itself. The stress of being back at work is not conducive to this healing. You must take exceptional care during this time. June 1 is the earliest you can possibly hope to return to work."

Bam! That door slammed shut. And a memory came back to me instantly. It was the image of my brain as a baby, swaddled in a blanket in my arms. This vision was from before I had quit work to become a massage therapist. It told me to settle down and listen to my doctor. I relented and resigned myself to the decision. I called Trish back and let her know there would be no change to my start date.

It seemed I would have the next two and a half months to figure out my new life. The next day, I had my first outing on my own—to the grocery store. I walked to the nearest store, which was under half a mile from my apartment. It was terrifying.

I lived on a very busy street and because I walked on the left side of the street, this put all the traffic to my right. Cars coming towards me approached from the center of my vision, so I could see them coming and watch them disappear into my blind spot. Cars coming from the rear would magically appear once they were past my blind spot. Since there was a very wide sidewalk, I walked on the far left-hand side to put the traffic as far away as possible. I only crossed at the signalized intersections. I knew I was relatively safe, but I still felt very vulnerable.

Once in the store, I was in for a surprise. The first thing I needed was peanut butter. Looking at the shelves, I was stunned. I wanted a certain brand of natural peanut butter, but I could not tell them apart in the mob of peanut butter options. I searched frantically, looking at the impossibly huge number of choices, not able to see the one I wanted. I finally found a jar with the word "natural" on it, grabbed it, and thrust it into the grocery cart. It was not the exact brand I wanted, but my heart was racing, and I was self-conscious about standing there for over five minutes looking at peanut butter.

This happened with each item I needed. I grabbed the first thing that was at all close to what I wanted, instead of searching for the exact item. As I was passing through the juice section, I was surprised and excited to find my vision resting on a brand of juice I loved. It was on sale, buy one get one free. I got two, mostly because this might be the only item in my cart that was the exact thing I wanted.

I went to check out with my eight items. When I got to the cashier, I found it difficult to understand the little box that credit cards are swiped through. I had used them a million times, yet I couldn't figure this one out. I had to ask the cashier what to do. "I'm sorry, I have a visual impairment and can't really understand this well," I told her. She was very kind and helped me get my purchase completed.

Next, I discovered my mistake in buying juice. It didn't occur to me how heavy the two half-gallon glass jars would be. The walk home was arduous, carrying my two bags of groceries.

I made it home, unlocked the door, put the bags of groceries on the floor, and collapsed on the couch, exhausted yet exhilarated. In spite of all the difficulties, I was extremely proud of myself—I had done it! I made a mental note to limit my grocery runs on my own to a weight that I could easily carry home, and then I congratulated myself on getting out of the apartment alone and conquering my first mission.

After this, I started going on daily walks. I was becoming much more comfortable with being out in the wide-open spaces. I started to realize I would not be able to see everything, so I needed to just pay attention to areas from which danger could arise. I became at ease with having things happen that I did not see or comprehend. The important thing was to know where cars were coming and going, and that I was not in their paths.

In the morning, when I planned out my day, if there were no errands I needed to "walk," I would get on the bike path by my apartment and go for at least an hour walk. Afterwards, I felt alive and inspired. Exercise was my brain's friend. The endorphins I had experienced in working out before were more noticeable now. My brain was so delicate and, frequently, depleted. The increased blood flow and enhancement of mood-altering hormones perked it up and made me more at ease.

After a few days of idyllic conquests, there was a bump in the road. My neurologist had prescribed occupational therapy to help me learn to cope with my visual impairment. She indicated that I would learn methods to lessen the impact of my disability on my life. I hoped they would help me learn to grocery shop better!

I happened to have a lunch engagement the day of my occupational therapy appointment, the next Wednesday morning. Knowing I would have a busy morning, and not wanting to have to coordinate too many trips on RTD, Denver's public transit system, I asked my lunch date to give me a ride to and from lunch. I thought I had done a great job of mitigating any potential stress.

On Tuesday afternoon, I began planning my first transit trip. I went on the RTD website and printed off the step-by-step instructions for going to the appointment and coming home. I put the large packet in a folder in my backpack. The travel estimate was a little over an hour to go eight miles. I was excited and a little nervous. Tomorrow would be my biggest day since coming home from the hospital.

I had an early dinner, then got to bed. I wanted to get plenty of sleep, and I would be getting up at 6:30 the next morning.

The alarm went off, and I trudged out of bed. It was the first time I'd used an alarm in a month, since before I went to Costa Rica at the end of February. I looked outside, and it was snowing to beat the band. I'd need to dress excessively warmly, as I had to transfer busses, and it was a fifteen-minute wait at the transfer point.

I slugged back the rest of my coffee, ate the last bite of my bagel, and found an extra layer of clothing, which I put on. Then I grabbed my backpack and scooted out the door, making the short walk to the bus stop. I learned a lot about transit that day. My first bus was late, so when I arrived at the transfer stop, there was no one waiting there. I had missed the bus to which I was transferring and had to wait for the next bus on that route. I had no idea how long that would be under good circumstances. The bus finally arrived, and I got to my appointment late, only to find out the kind of therapy I needed was not offered through my insurance.

Exhausted and crushed, I could not face another transit ride, so I texted my lunch date. I asked if it were possible to pick me up at the medical offices where my appointment had been. It was, so I snuggled into a chair for the wait.

Lunch was nice, but when I was dropped at home, I knew I had overdone it drastically. I went straight to bed and slept for four hours.

When I awoke at six o'clock, I was still exhausted, and incredibly distraught. It seemed this stroke was a much larger life change than I had anticipated. I searched for any tinge of optimism I might be able to muster, but there was none. A dark, silver-lining-less cloud hung over my head and, try as I might, I could not dissipate it.

My sense of hopelessness was pervasive. I had struggled with depression at times in my life, but this was something altogether different. I wasn't even energetic enough to feel depressed.

The day's disappointments and frustrations came spilling back to me. First, the frustration of the bus ride—not knowing if busses had already come or would come. Having budgeted an extra half hour in my eight-mile commute, only to be late. Then arriving to find I had wasted my time and my insurance would provide no help for me. I searched for something good to occupy my mind, but the victory of navigating my first transit trip felt like defeat.

I began to cry with frustration and fear, which brought more of both. My thoughts tumbled out of my head like a never-ending stream of dice from a cup. *What was I going to do? Transit sucked and was so undependable. What would happen when I had to get to work every day? Or, heaven forbid, what if I couldn't get to work every day? What if I couldn't even work? What if they fired me? What if I had another stroke? What if...... Stop!*

Be reasonable, I told myself. *It can't be so bad, what are you really worried about?* And the answer came: *I can't plan anything. I have two and a half months to figure out my life, and I can't plan a single thing! I don't know how my life will turn out, or what to do about anything.*

I decided going to bed was the perfect thing to do. I slept for what seemed ages, waking only to go to the restroom, get a drink of water and a bite of something to eat, and to note the feeling of crushing doom upon me. Then back to bed to sleep for several more hours.

I awoke a day and a half later, feeling rested and myself again. I thought back to my fear of not being able to plan my life. And a small voice inside me said, *Look, you thought you had your whole life planned out on February 28, and on March 1, all of those plans were gone. Can you ever, really, plan anything? No, you simply develop options.* So, I started to develop options.

There was a business side of my new life to figure out. Trish had sent me a packet of information on short-term and long-term disability, which arrived right after I got home from the hospital. When I had received it, I thought Trish was being unnecessarily bureaucratic. I had resisted the urge to toss it in the trash and stashed it in a file cabinet. I dragged the packet out now and, looking through it, I made a list of steps to take. I decided to do one each day, but for today, making the list was enough.

The next day, I called the short-term disability insurance agent and inquired how all of this worked. I was told short-term disability insurance would take effect after I'd been off the job for thirty days. I would be paid for this first thirty days off, since I had exactly the amount of sick leave it took to cover the waiting period. On April 1, short-term disability insurance would kick in and pay me up to 60 percent of my pre-disability salary. And, unless I was eligible for disability leave from my pension, they would continue paying this amount for up to three months, or until June 30.

"I'm returning to work half-time on June 1," I told the insurance agent.

"Then for the month of June, you will only receive 50 percent from us. We make your pay whole for any time you miss from work, but only up to 100 percent." I felt relieved.

The next day, I called my pension to see if I were eligible to receive any assistance from them. The man I spoke to was very helpful and informative. He said I would be eligible for disability from my pension after I had *actually worked* at WI for five years. The time I had purchased did not count in this case. I needed to remain in paid status until April 1 to qualify, as I had started back to work with Winfrow on April 1, five years ago. Interestingly, that was exactly what was going to happen, because I was in paid status while on sick leave for thirty days.

My pension's disability program became effective after a sixty-day waiting period from the date upon which I became eligible. I told the gentleman I was returning to work half-time starting June 1 and would be paid by disability insurance through July 1.

He said, "Starting June 1, the pension will replace short-term disability, paying up to 60 percent of your pre-disability pay, for as long as you are deemed to be on short-term disability. If you are never able to return to work full-time, then we will have to investigate putting you on disability retirement. That would take about a year to work out. If it were approved, you would get 50 percent of your pay for life. "

I hung up, wrote copious notes about what I had discovered, and quit for the day. I needed my walk to clear my head and reinvigorate my brain.

The next day, I organized the notes of the previous day's conversation:

1. I would be paid my full salary for the month of March, due to being on sick leave.

2. Short-term disability insurance would pay me 60 percent of my pay for the months of April and May. I would be short 40 percent for these two months. I had no savings, because I had been putting all my money into my retirement plan.

3. Starting June 1, until I was released from short-term disability, I would continue receiving half my pay from my wages and the other half through my pension.

4. Disability retirement?

I sat back and looked at this. It was fascinating, and a little eerie, to see how all the puzzle pieces fit together seamlessly. I became eligible for disability benefits (had worked for WI again for five years to the day) on March 31, or the last day of my leave usage—the last day I would actually be working for WI and paying into the pension plan—until June. If I'd had the stroke earlier, I would not have gained access to this payment. Between the two types of insurance, I would only be out 40 percent of my pay for two months.

Was this a coincidence? I had a strong feeling it was not. With this thought, I felt an intuition growing inside of me. I knew there was something meaningful happening in my life, and I felt it would be revealed to me over time. I wasn't quite certain what to think about the representative bringing up disability retirement, other than it was a bit premature.

The next concern was to figure out a budget for those two months when I would be paid 60 percent of my paycheck. I felt overwhelmed with the idea of making a budget for myself. I couldn't understand why. It had nothing to do with vision, but trying to think of the complex steps involved paralyzed me. I thought briefly about the irony of the situation. I used to produce such elaborate and extensive budgets for my job, but now I couldn't even think of what it entailed to examine my tiny household budget.

I remembered in February, I had still been contributing $2,000 per month to my retirement plan. I stopped this immediately, so my March paycheck would not be diminished by this amount. In addition, I decided to charge all the expenses I could on a credit card. Then, I would simply pay the bills and see how it all worked out. If I didn't have enough money to pay the credit cards in full, I would pay them down slowly starting in June, when I started receiving 100 percent of my salary again.

I could relax, I had developed some options that were completely reasonable, and I was going to be able to keep my finances afloat through my recovery. I felt very blessed.

Journal entry:

April 1, 2013

It didn't really strike me at first that today is April Fools' Day. It's something much more important. A milestone. One month since my stroke. One month ago, my life changed and for one month I've dealt with those changes. Is one month a short time or a long time? Both. It's short because the days have melted into one another and they become one very long, monotonous day, punctuated with many poignant moments.

But it also seems like a long time. I've been through many phases in this time. There were the first few days, when I was insanely optimistic, hearing what I wanted to hear from the doctors, seeing what I wanted to see in my brain's optical illusions of sight. I was going to be back behind the wheel and at work in a couple of weeks. I've read emails I wrote in those first days, and I'm dismayed at my ability to ignore the obvious. They call it denial, but I felt like I was in acceptance. I was in acceptance of denial.

This was many of my friends' favorite phase. We could all believe the fairy tale together and there was no discomfort and no facing of problems and nothing any of us had to think about. It was a pretty picture and it felt good to look at it. People don't like it when you make them think about things which are ugly or messy. Some tried to get me to stay in this phase.

Then there was a new phase with the prognosis by my neurologist: there would be no recovery. This was a stark reality. For a few hours, there was a sickening stomachache that said, "You knew this all along. You said it to the kids the first night. Your intuition predicted this, but you ignored it."

Next, I went quickly through whatever those other phases are. Depression? Check! Bargaining? I don't think I did bargaining. I gave up bargaining a long time ago. It's too much like begging. It's pitiful. I try not to do pitiful. Grieving? Yes, I grieved intermittently. Not so much for my vision or the other things I lost, but more giving up the life I'd planned, and the uncertainty in the life that was waiting for me. There's another phase in there, but I don't remember what it is.

Then we come to acceptance again. Some days, acceptance is easy. It isn't even a thing; it just is. I get up and I do the things I must do, and I never even think about if it's different, or if it's good or bad. It just is. This is my life. Other days, the shoe doesn't fit as comfortably. My blind spot gives me problems and I want lunch at Chipotle, but I don't want a two-mile walk for it, and I want to know where I'll live and what I'll do and what I'll be like in two months. I want help, but I want to be fiercely independent. But whether I accept with ease, or I struggle with acceptance, these days pass and suddenly it is one month down the road, and the phases are still changing, but not so dramatically.

When I meditate, I feel better. I chant to Ganesh [the Yogic and Hindu remover of obstacles] and imagine the elephant god removing barriers in my path for the moment, the day, the week, and my lifetime. And I imagine Lakshmi [the goddess of abundance and contentment], placing opportunities to feel abundance along my path. Yes, my path is being set in a fortuitous manner. I concentrate on my breath and the feeling of goodness that comes from it. I feel better.

[Written later in the day.]

I decided to make soup, which means I had to go to the store and leave this reverie. I walked toward the grocery store, but along the way, I was compelled to go a little further to the coffee shop and have a latte and sit in the sunshine. It's a beautiful Colorado day and it will be cold again tomorrow, so I wanted to savor it. I sat, thoroughly enjoying my soy latte and the warmth of the sun on my skin.

I heard, "You made it to Starbucks!" and I looked around to see a woman and a young man, who was holding a cane. I remembered the first day I left the house without a chauffeur and I walked to the grocery store, frightened and alone. I bought a few things, went home, and I was incredibly proud of myself. I was drawn from the contemplation of my coffee as I heard the woman describe the surroundings to the young man. She told him where the chairs were, and talked to him about the street nearby, the traffic sounds that might trick him because they were parallel to the parking lot.

I decided to leave and they left simultaneously. I walked partway home behind them. I remembered to be grateful for the blessings bestowed upon me in my stroke. I still have enough vision to tell the difference between traffic on a street, twenty feet away, and traffic in the parking lot nearby. Unlike some people who've had a stroke, I can still walk and talk and live independently. I am alive and enjoying a latte and feeling the warm sun on my skin. Yes, in this moment, I can completely accept this life. I love this life.

I paid very close attention to find lessons the Universe might be offering me. Perhaps this stroke was comparable to when I was a grant specialist and I needed to learn the lessons to move to the next phase. True or not, I learned a lot that helped me adjust to my circumstances. I learned many lessons—big and small.

The small ones were things like, if at all possible, invest the time to go to a signalized intersection to cross the street. You can only depend upon drivers, whose cars are in your blind spot, slamming on their brakes and narrowly avoiding you, for so long. I learned stopping and feeling the sun on my face is a beautiful thing, and to do it often. I learned, if I bundled up correctly, walking in a driving snow at twelve degrees Fahrenheit wasn't nearly as bad as the consequences of not getting my daily walk. I learned sometimes, even though you've worked on finding contentment in a difficult situation, in the end it is still a difficult situation and it's okay to grieve.

I learned when you're a little sad, you can find hundreds of standup comics to watch for free. In fact, standup comedy was the easiest way for me to watch television—partially because I didn't have cable television, and comedy was plentiful on streaming services. Standup comedy was nice because it cheered me up, and the person generally stood still in the middle of the screen. Because of this, I could easily follow what was happening, and it didn't tire my brain as quickly as shows with lots of action.

During this time, I developed a huge crush on a certain comedian—one might even say I was obsessed. It was odd, because he didn't have the physical characteristics to which I was normally attracted, which were dark hair, eyes, and complexion, and an athletic build. Although I was generally attracted to funny guys, this man's humor was more brash than I would have expected to enjoy. But enjoy it I did. I watched all his standup, and when I started to feel comfortable watching shows with more movement, I watched every episode of his series. I looked him up on the internet to see if he were doing live shows and if there was a possibility I could meet him. I hadn't had an obsession like this since I was eight and fell in love with Donny Osmond (a member of one of the first "boy bands"—The Osmond Brothers—from the '70s).

The lesson of the exhaustion spell was the biggest lesson of all. If I didn't get enough good food, physical activity, and rest, there was hell to pay with my brain. If I overdid it slightly, I would have an evening of inconsolable sobbing. There was no getting out of this. No joke could make me laugh, no memory of a fun time could bring me joy, no amount of thinking about how much more fortunate I was than some others could assuage my sorrow. The only thing to do was to cry uncontrollably for about three hours, then collapse in a snotty, tear-streaked, exhausted pile of flesh and sleep for fifteen or more hours. This, I realized now, was what had happened to me the day of my first bus outing. I couldn't understand, at the time, why I was so inconsolable. Then, I slept for a day and a half and felt fine. I had had a mini exhaustion spell.

If I didn't heed the mini exhaustion warning signs and continued to abuse my brain, I got the full-strength exhaustion spell. My first experience of this was in mid-April. I was starting to get used to my new life and take for granted feeling good. And maybe I was rebelling against my limitations as well, searching for my boundaries like a teenager trying out defiance for the first time.

On this particular day, I didn't want to go for my walk, so I skipped it. Then I tried to get through all my mail by myself. Jake usually came over once a week and helped me read things I had problems with. But I decided I could do it. I worked on the five or six pieces of mail for two hours, straining to read items that turned out to be unimportant. In frustration, I turned on the TV to distract myself from the dull heaviness that had started in my head. I watched a one-hour comedy show, staying up about fifteen minutes later than normal. The comedy didn't seem funny at all, and in what I thought was a foul mood, I got ready for bed and fell asleep as soon as my head hit the pillow.

I awoke the next morning still feeling awful. The heaviness in my brain, which made it feel like my thoughts were occurring in slow motion, was still there. I had an appointment, though, so I made myself get up and go.

I returned in the afternoon, feeling lethargic. I laid down on the couch, and I was incapable of movement. I slept—well, not actually slept—more like became unconscious for hours at a time. Occasionally, I regained consciousness dreadfully, wearily, groggily, and only for long enough to visit the bathroom, drink a glass of water, or maybe eat a bite of something. Then back to unconsciousness.

It was abject misery, although I cannot say why I was so miserable. The experience wasn't painful, except in the way when you wake from a very sound sleep and your brain won't work. I woke, and simply to rouse myself and figure out why I woke up, where I was, and how to make my body sit up was a huge effort. I stumbled the five feet to use the bathroom, got a drink of water, and struggled to remain awake long enough to get back to the couch, where I again became unconscious.

In the few waking moments, I wondered what was wrong with me. Was this depression? No, it wasn't depression; it was oppression. It was hard to move—my body felt lifeless and difficult to get going. It was even harder to think. The only coherent thought that would come out of the fog surrounding me was, "I wish I were dead." This thought was with me when I was conscious and finding the bathroom, some water, a little food, and it was with me when I was unconscious.

There were no dreams and I didn't feel rested upon waking. I absolutely felt like I should die. This went on for three days—being unconscious for about twenty hours of each day.

As the exhaustion spell began to subside on the third day, I was awake for a little longer. Not able to think or do anything, but not unconscious. During this time, I sat on the couch, without the energy to turn on the TV or ponder what I would like to eat. I simply sat there, staring into space, listening to my brain repeat to me, "I wish I were dead." The misery and the thought of death were the only things I had.

On day four, I "came to." I woke feeling rested and normal again. I was happy, and I had no idea why I had wanted to die mere hours before. I vowed to never go through an exhaustion spell again and I would carefully guard against getting over-tired. And I did a good job, to the extent I could control what was happening in my life.

I had tried to have healthy habits before the stroke, but I was learning the need to take care of myself was paramount now. I walked to the store every other day and bought fresh produce. Returning home, I'd put on some relaxing music to set a nice mood for my food preparation. In my one-person galley kitchen, I washed the colorful vegetables. Getting out the cutting board and knife, I reminded myself to be careful. If I were looking at the zucchini in my left hand, I couldn't see the knife in my right. Trying to perform the rapid-cutting action of chefs on television was a thing of the past.

I learned to go to bed when I got sleepy, even if it were seven o'clock, and I slept until I was rested. I deliberately left my schedule open for two hours every afternoon, in case I needed a nap. This was a stark contrast to the life where five hours of sleep was a luxury, and I frequently got up at two a.m. to complete the work I hadn't done in my previous ten- to twelve-hour workday.

I learned I needed a moderate amount of physical activity every day, and I guarded my regimen carefully. On the rare occasions when I could not get my exercise in, I learned to not obsess about it. In addition, moderate exercise now meant my three-mile walk, and an occasional yoga class, not a six a.m. yoga class before work, a run after work, and cleaning house until midnight after dinner. These were very important things for me to learn before I went back to work—the environment where my old, bad habits seemed to be a requirement.

I began learning how my brain worked post-stroke. I discovered once something simple was in my brain, my brain worked the same as it did before. If the concept wasn't too complicated, I could consider options; think things through; make good decisions; and be quite insightful. It was exponentially more difficult to get these things *into* my brain, however.

On the other hand, putting ideas together, whether presented in writing, orally, or in my own mind, was incredibly difficult. My stroke had begun in my cerebellum, the communication center for the brain, and sometimes it felt like the different parts of my brain didn't speak the same language. Thoughts were disjointed, and concepts others understood instantaneously didn't make sense to me.

Before the stroke, I had packed a bag for work each day, which included my work clothes (because I started my day at a yoga class and showered there), foods for breakfast, lunch and sometimes dinner, clothing for a post-work run, then something to wear while getting together with friends for happy hour, and any other events that might occur in the time I was gone from home. Now, I had trouble figuring out what I needed to take to walk to the grocery store and stop off for a coffee on the way.

I had problems with spatial relationships, which encompassed varied aspects of life. Managing a calendar might not seem like a spatial endeavor, but I was not able to understand the layers of activities and how they coincided with life outside of the schedule grids.

I put things on the calendar in order of the time they were to occur, like anyone else. But in deciding how to proceed with my day, I wouldn't understand how the flow of time worked. I didn't even understand how it happened, but I would make intricate plans for how to get somewhere on time—which meant planning to be there half an hour early if I were taking RTD—only to have everything go exactly as planned and arrive after the appointment had begun. Then, I'd look back at the bus schedule, or think about the timing and realize there was an error in logic there. But it had been perfectly logical to me when I'd planned it.

I even lost a friend over one of these situations. Dave had made plans with me for the afternoon of Tuesday after next, and my friend Dina and I planned a long lunch on April 23. The Tuesday after next happened to be April 23. I put both my dates with Dina and Dave on my calendar, and somehow it didn't occur to me this wouldn't work.

Each evening, I would put together a transportation plan for the following day, printing out bus schedules I would need, or confirming rides I had requested from friends. When I sat down on Monday, April 22, it was clear something had to give for the next day. Dave had already paid for tickets to an event, so I had to cancel on Dina, with whom I had planned lunch.

Unfortunately, this was the second time this had happened with her. When I apologized for my error and cancelled our lunch date, she retorted, "Well, you let me know when I fit into your busy social calendar."

I tried to explain what happened, but it was difficult, since I didn't really understand it myself. In the end, I made a difficult decision. If she couldn't be more understanding of my issues, then she simply didn't fit into my social calendar, or life, at all. When she didn't reply to my apology and attempt at resolution, I stopped trying. I didn't contact her again, nor did she contact me.

I was never totally certain, but it seemed to me as if Dina thought I was exaggerating my issues. When she had visited me a few weeks after my stroke, she had mentioned her legally blind vision in one eye a couple of times. She could drive and read just fine, she told me. Why couldn't I? She, not unnaturally, equated having extremely poor vision in one eye to my problem, which was completely different. I could never adequately explain to her why having a brain injury that wiped out half of my visual interpretation in both eyes, plus disrupted my cognitive processes, was different than her visual impairment.

My issue was not easily understood, or visible to an observer. I was frustrated to realize someone who had been a long-time friend would choose her own opinion, rather than believe what I told her. I wondered how many people would choose this course of action. I felt embarrassed that some of my co-workers might doubt my need to be away from work for three months, or even disbelieve I had an issue at all. I knew I needed to get past caring about what "some people" might think.

I was learning to deal with another, more notably spatial, issue: geography. I had always been geographically challenged, but now I couldn't understand how to transfer the limited geographical knowledge I had to real-world applications.

On the way home from the coffee shop, there was an intersection where I needed to go from the southeast corner to the northwest corner. Since the stroke, I had always crossed west first, then north. But one day, the light at the pedestrian crossing was red going west, and green going north. It was more efficient to cross northerly first, so I did. When I arrived at the northeast corner of the intersection, I suddenly had no idea where I was. I was in an area where I had lived, shopped, and driven for twenty-eight years. I recognized landmarks. There was the office of the insurance agent I'd used for almost two decades; there was the movie theatre that had been built fifteen years ago; there, across the street, was the shop where I'd had coffee moments ago.

But where was the way home? I had no idea. I started walking along the sidewalk, in what I later discovered was the wrong direction. Soon, I came to the side of the grocery store where I always shopped. I wondered, *If I go inside the store, when I come out, will I know where I am?* I tried this strategy, and it worked. But it was terrifying to be lost in my own neighborhood.

Reading was difficult, thus Jake's weekly visit to help me read my mail, or whatever I saved because I couldn't understand it. I also could not scan a document for information. Before the stroke, I could magically skip over bits of information in a document that were unimportant to me, and then begin reading more intently when I came to the part that was of interest. It amazed me to remember this was ever possible.

I discovered my lack of scanning acuity when looking at a directory of offices in a building. I tried looking for the name of the office I wanted, which started with "Neuro." I skimmed the whole directory, and it wasn't there. I called the business and they gave me their suite number, then I looked at the directory to see how they had disguised the name. I read each suite number until I got to theirs, then looked at the name next to it. There it was, "Neurosculpting Institute," as plain as day.

I figured out I must read every word, instead of scanning, to find the information for which I was searching. I read impossibly slowly anyway, and this impediment slowed me down even further. When given something to read in the presence of others, I would simply put it aside and say, "I'll read this later," as I had instinctively at the hospital when visitors gave me get well cards.

In the last several years before the stroke, I had figured out how to be alone incredibly well. With the disappointment of my relationships since the divorce, I had resigned myself to solitude, and had designed my life around being single forever. But since the stroke, when I was worried, or confused, or grieving, what I wished for most was someone to hold me. The saddest part for me was that I had no one to go through this with me. Sure, I had friends and family who were happy to help me occasionally, but I had no one who was truly invested in my life, who *lived* my problems with me.

I remembered joking with my friend at work—what seemed decades ago—about how I would find a man with a huge house, cable television, and NFL ticket. I now added to my wish list: he needed to be sweet, compassionate, and love to cuddle with me.

The very most important thing I learned was to be thankful for what I had. I was grateful I had both health insurance and short-term disability insurance in place when the stroke occurred; grateful I had decreased my cost of living, and now I could live within what I received from the disability insurance. I was grateful I had the love of friends and family. I was grateful my stroke had not been worse—I was able to walk out of the hospital, and I could still be physically active. Mostly, I was grateful to feel an assurance that everything would be okay.

24

In May, at the urging of my neurologist, I decided to see a mental health therapist. I made an appointment through my employee assistance program. The date of my appointment was a lovely Colorado day, and the commute downtown, via light rail, was relatively easy. The office was in a high-rise, a few steps from the light rail stop.

I arrived quite early, since my commute had gone smoothly, so I anticipated a long wait. They were able to take me back right away, though. I sat in the awkward room, which looked more like an accountant's office than that of a therapist. The large desk was the main focal point, with a very small seating area, with two stuffed chairs in a corner.

Giovanna walked into the room—she was young and slender, with long dark hair. Her poise and confidence were far beyond her very young appearance. She sat at the desk, which I was sitting near, and asked what had brought me in. I told her about the stroke, and my neurologist's suggestion of counseling. She asked if I would be more comfortable where we were sitting, or if I'd like to move to the sitting area. We moved over to the comfy chairs and started our session.

We talked about my fear of some people at work thinking I was exaggerating my disability and bilking the system. How I was adjusting to losing the freedom of driving. How I had been a life-long voracious reader and I missed being able to read effortlessly.

The most important issue of all was my desire for a romantic life-partner. I admitted I ached to have someone to lean upon. I hoped she would tell me how to be tougher and get through this without feeling this need to be supported. But instead, she asked, "Are you actively dating?"

I was shocked by the impracticality of her question. "Of course not. The huge amount of baggage I have would be too much to unload on anyone."

One of her eyebrows raised as she asked, "What baggage are you talking about?"

"Well, I've had a stroke. I can't drive a car, read a book, or shop for groceries. I don't know how this will all end up. Maybe I won't be able to do my job or support myself. Maybe I will have to move closer to transit. What if I have another stroke and things are even worse? My whole life is up in the air right now."

Then she said the most preposterous thing. "Did it ever occur to you, perhaps, you'd meet someone who would be so loving and caring this wouldn't be baggage to him?"

"No, it has never even occurred to me that such a person might exist."

She could tell I was very resistant to the idea, so she let it go for the time being. We talked more about how I was managing my new life. Giovanna was impressed with the way I was moving forward, saying my coping mechanisms and adaptation strategies were primarily healthy. Her feedback gave me confidence in my thoughts on how to proceed during my recovery. I left the appointment with three assignments: to ask for help *even more;* to process my feelings about how others perceived me and work towards accepting that what others think of me is none of my business; and to think about dating.

I resolved to consciously ask for help more often (I had struggled a few times with getting to appointments and resisted asking for help). I made a list of items I could have delivered instead of getting them myself. Some grocery stores were starting to have delivery services, and I could order many things online. I thought going to the grocery store was good for me and planned to do most of my shopping myself. But it would be nice to have things delivered when I had a taxing week, or I needed some heavy things. This would allow me to ask for help yet feel independent at the same time. My life would be much easier if I accepted these conveniences, instead of insisting on doing most things myself.

As for processing my feelings about how others perceived me, I knew I had grown a lot over the last two months in this area. I was better at resisting my friends' needs to put their issues in dealing with my condition on me. They wanted to believe nothing had changed—I was now "back to normal"—and they wanted me to act as if they were correct.

When I would express difficulties created by my disability, they'd say, "But everything's all better now, right?" When I told them it was not, they would usually say, "But you look great—exactly like you did before." I wanted to scream at them. How I looked had nothing to do with anything! During the entire stroke itself, and ever since, I *looked* the same as I had before the stroke. The issues were inside my brain, not on my face or in my arms and legs.

I had friends who had similar issues with "hidden" diseases, such as early stage multiple sclerosis, fibromyalgia, lupus, even grieving over the death of a child that happened years ago. I sought them out. We shared the experience of the general fruitlessness of saying anything to most people about what we were feeling, and what our current lives were really about. It was comforting to know this was commonplace, and not simply a failure of my friends to grasp my reality. These conversations helped me to develop my own ideas to meet this situation head-on.

It seemed most people had already made up their minds about all of this and my reality did not matter to them. My friends visited with me because they cared about me, but they really cared about the me who died on March 1. The me who survived was unknown and perhaps a little scary for them. I couldn't play the part in their lives I had played before. We had to find a new way of relating.

By necessity, I decided to relegate these people to a lesser part of my life or cut them out entirely. Like Dina, whose friendship could not withstand comparing her visual disability to mine. Some of them even cut me out of *their* lives. Before, I would have searched for ways to bring them back, to make myself acceptable to them. But now, I didn't have the energy to carry my issues as well as theirs. They didn't understand I still embodied the soul of the other person within me, and she still had the same ambition, desire, strength, feistiness, and joie de vivre that I had always had. They might not understand I had to temper all these qualities with more patience, caution, acceptance, and love for myself. I was still growing and learning who I would become. I needed friends who would do their part to help me discover how we would grow together and incorporate these changes into our relationship.

I made good progress on my first two homework assignments from Giovanna. But I hit a wall with the dating idea. How could I manage a new relationship when I was having trouble managing the ones I already had? How could I expect someone I was meeting for the first time to understand something I couldn't get through to people who already knew and cared about me? Dating would need to be put off for a while longer.

I saw Giovanna once a week during May. I would wait until I had gone back to work to judge how frequently I could make the downtown trek to see her while managing my half-time work schedule.

As my prescribed three-month hiatus from work slipped by, I started to realize it was possible I would not be able to do my job anymore. However, I hadn't processed the idea enough to understand what this information might mean, if it were true. At my next appointment, I brought it up with Giovanna. I told her I was afraid of not being able to do my job. If I were unable to go back to work, my life would be horrible.

"What about your life right now, during your three months off? Has it been so horrible?"

"No, I wouldn't say horrible. Definitely different. But I can't live the rest of my life like this." I had never, in these two and a half months since the stroke, imagined my current life might be my entire future.

"Why not?"

"I don't know," I said, but I did know, because the next thing out of my mouth was, "I don't want to be disabled. I don't want people to think of me that way." Then, I quickly added, "Oh, geez! There I go with what other people think of me again. I thought I'd worked through that."

My wise young therapist told me, "I think you've worked through the first few layers of the issue. Now, we come to a new one. But this one seems to be more than just what others think. What do *you* think about you being disabled?"

"I've never used that word out loud about myself. I'm not disabled, I'm just recovering."

Giovanna smiled knowingly. "But you're unable to drive because of your visual impairment. You told me reading and complex thoughts are difficult because of your cognitive deficiencies. Aren't those aspects of having a disability?"

I couldn't speak, and she didn't fill the space with conversation for me. We sat for a few moments, with me pondering her impactful statement. I started to cry, and she handed me a box of tissues. But the silence was only broken by my sniffling.

I felt the need to say something, anything, to end the silence. "Okay, I guess I have a disability right now."

We discussed my changing definition of myself, how I knew I was not the same as before the stroke. "Disability" was simply a label, not a prison sentence. It was a shorter way of saying I have a visual impairment and cognitive difficulties. I didn't have to refer to myself with the word, but I needed to be prepared that it did describe one facet of my life. One very important facet.

"Why would you want to make your life painful, or even dangerous, to avoid a label?"

"I…I don't know," I whispered.

"Let's revisit my question from earlier. What is your life like right now, as a disabled person who is not working?"

"It's okay. I am busy all the time. I have to walk to the store, so I go every other day. I cook and clean and occasionally watch a little TV. I need my long walk every day to feel good. My brain needs a lot of sleep, so I do that. I meditate a lot and go to yoga whenever I want. I'm never bored or run out of things to do."

"Do you enjoy your life right now?"

"Actually, most of the time, I do. Wow, that's interesting to admit. I really do enjoy my life right now."

"So, what would happen if you continued to enjoy your life, and reserved judgment about your future life until you find out what that is?"

Silence ensued again as I contemplated this thought. Then I realized, "I guess I'd be happy," which was quite a revelation—that I could have a disability *and* be happy. "The one thing that doesn't make me happy is, all those things I do, I do alone," I said. "I still want a boyfriend, but the idea of dating is awful."

"Do you think, if you became more comfortable with how your life is, as a person with a disability, and what your life will be, once you know about work, you would be more comfortable dating?"

"Probably," was all I could say. We were near the end of our time, and my brain was beginning to buzz. I knew enough about my "disability" to know that meant I needed to stop this intense thinking, get myself home, and get a nap. We ended a few minutes early, and I did just that.

After a two-hour nap, I was refreshed and eager to assimilate the information from my session. I knew the idea of a boyfriend could wait. I hadn't had a true life-partner in fourteen years; I could defer those thoughts a little longer while I awaited the outcomes of going back to work and the passage of time. It was a relief to put this idea on the shelf for now, knowing I would be ready soon, and then it would happen.

As for work itself, I would be going back in two weeks, and that would be soon enough to start grappling with whether I could do the job or not. Giovanna had helped me understand, if I couldn't do the job, I could still live a good life, which my future boyfriend and I would enjoy together.

The one thing I knew with brilliant clarity was this: I could never completely be the pre-stroke me again. I felt I'd been put on this path for a purpose and the purpose was becoming known to me little by little, in microscopic pieces. The new purpose was drastically different than the purpose of the previous Laurie. My new purpose would require the skills and discipline and passion that I had learned in my old life, but they would be used in a new and magical fashion. I was beginning to have a feeling of anticipation, which was quite beautiful and so strong. I was excited to see where this path would lead me, while remaining a little scared of how I would get there.

On Saturday, June 1, I was released from most of the limitations my doctor placed on me. I could return to work part-time, and it was magically safe for me to put my head below my heart again. The new me was about to find out what it was like to step back into my old life.

My first act of freedom was to do hot yoga again. I had done only "non-hot" yoga class since the day of the stroke. The class was blissfully amazing. I felt free from all the effects, thoughts, desires, and fears that had plagued me over the last three months. I felt normal, but in a new way. I felt like I was me again. I was not contrasting the old me to the new me, but simply being me. If being able to do yoga and feel whole had been taken from me, I didn't know how I'd have been able to get through life.

On the walk home from class, I texted Jake and told him how wonderful I felt and how blessed I was to have no aspect of the stroke touch my physical being. His text back said, simply, "I'm so happy for you, Momma."

Sunday night, I went online and used RTD's website to figure out how I would get home from work. A lovely friend had contacted me and offered a ride to work. She offered a ride home as well, but I felt I needed to start gaining in confidence and independence with my transit adventures, so I declined the ride home.

Again, I printed out reams of paper. I printed the route I should take, but I had learned it was a good idea to print the schedules of each of the buses and the train that I needed, in case I missed a connection. My commute when I'd driven had taken twenty minutes, at most, but I would make the transit trip in a little over an hour, if all went as planned.

I suddenly remembered something a former boyfriend had told me. Don was paralyzed from a motorcycle accident and we had dated for about six months. He told me the biggest thing he learned after the accident was that things would simply take longer than they had before. I accepted this new fact of my life, noting how the Universe had moved in a direction, over ten years ago, which provided a perfect message for me today.

When I went back to work on Monday I was terrified, which seemed odd because I was going back to people who I knew loved me and wanted the best for me. Jennie gave me a ride to work, and the nervousness fell away as soon as I got in the car. Jennie is perhaps *the* funniest person on earth, and laughing is mandatory in her presence. She dropped me at the entrance right next to my office and told me to call her if I changed my mind about the ride home.

I slipped into my office without being noticed. I sat down behind my desk and looked around. It was June 3, and I had not been to work since February 18. I had expected the nervousness to return, but it had subsided. Now, I felt nothing but a small amount of dread. I wasn't quite certain what to do, or where to start. I guessed I should check in with my boss.

As I started toward Bill's office, I met a woman—an acquaintance—in the hallway. "Oh, my God!" she exclaimed. "Laurie, you're back! You look great! It's so good to see you."

"Hi, it's great to be seen," I said, the stock answer I had developed in the hospital. "Thanks!"

"Wow! You're all better, already. That's so wonderful."

"Well, I'm not exactly all better."

"But you look the same as always."

"The damage to my brain isn't anything you can tell by looking at me. I am partially blind now and have some cognitive issues." I didn't really want to say this, not wanting to broadcast my medical challenges. But her cavalier attitude, and how she thought she could judge my life's ease or difficulty, after seeing me for thirty seconds, irritated me.

"Oh, but you're going to make a complete recovery, I'm sure. You look so healthy!"

I had the answer to my biggest concern—some people would not understand my disability because it was invisible to them. (I was getting more comfortable with the term disability.) I excused myself and went to the bathroom. I needed to process the confirmation her comments had given me before I met with Bill.

I calmed down easily. I had suspected this might happen, and now it had, so I was prepared. *Remember*, I told myself, *others' opinions are none of my business.* The mantra was a little hollow, but I knew I would practice it until it was true for me.

Leaving the ladies' room, I took a deep breath and prepared for the "front office." This was a cluster of offices and cubicles where all the executives and their assistants worked. I entered and was welcomed back with open arms. Everyone was very kind. Yet, for them, like the woman in the hallway, it was the same old Laurie coming back to do her job. For me, it was a whole new world, with email that would be hard to read, lights that shone too brightly and upset my brain, hordes of faces being thrust at me, a sense of defeat before I was even begun, and people's expectations stunning me with their lack of understanding of what was going on in my life. I smiled and kept reminding myself, even though they loved the old me, they would share the love with the new me, too.

After hugs, welcome backs, and "You look great!" from everyone, it was time to meet with my boss. I hadn't communicated with him for three months, other than to let him know what was going on right after the stroke. I needed to set boundaries and expectations—something I had learned to do in coping with my new life during my time off. I had never understood how to do this before.

"Welcome back," he said, "sit down." He offered a seat at his small conference table.

After the "how are you" platitudes, he got right down to business. "How do you want to move forward with returning to work?"

I hadn't really thought about it before, but it occurred to me it was best if things kept being done as they had been while I was gone, for now. I couldn't very well take over the more-than-full-time job while working half-time. The same person who had been doing the day-to-day management of my office needed to continue, except I would be present and discussing the decisions with him. I had to put my ego aside. I couldn't jump in and start making decisions and trying to catch up on everything that had happened in my absence. My office needed continuity, and I needed to guard against stressing myself out.

I expressed this to Bill, who was his usual, awkward, emotionless self. He agreed to what I had told him but had some follow-up questions.

"I'm not really allowed to ask you this, but do you think you'll ever be able to return to full-time work?" This was the opposite of the "I know you're fine" approach, and although it seemed like a heartless question, I knew Bill well enough to expect, and respect, it. He was trying to take care of my unit, which was what I wanted as well.

"I honestly have no idea. If it is possible, I will, but it will take time to know. I need to take care of my health first." This was a novel idea that I'd never tried before.

"Do you think you'll ever really be able to do your job again?"

"I've been asking myself that very question, and I truly do not know. I swing between thinking I'll come back and everything will be fine, and thinking it's a useless effort. I have not had the chance, need, or energy to even try to do anything like I do at work. I will do everything I possibly can. This is all I can tell you."

"Are you capable of thinking? I mean, this job requires a lot of critical thought, you know."

Now, I was getting impatient. "As I said, I have no idea. But my doctor and our pension say I should come back and try, so I shall come back and try my best. It is not my intention to run my unit into the ground. That's why I am suggesting I not take over right away. There would be too much disruption if I took over, then had to turn everything back. Give me a couple of weeks to see what I can do. If you have a better idea, feel free to tell me what it is."

We agreed we would go forward as I had suggested and meet again soon.

Next, I went back to my office, sat down at my desk, and opened my email to find thousands of unread messages. They were mostly from the first few weeks of March, when people were expecting me back from vacation and didn't know I'd had a stroke. I started looking at the titles, wondering how I would ever read and respond to them all. In the past, I would have felt the need to handle every one of the 4,700 emails I had received. It was good I had learned some lessons before I returned to work. I highlighted the entire mass of them and hit *Delete*. "Are you sure you want to delete?" my computer asked me. I wasn't sure of anything, but I took a deep breath and selected *Yes*.

I sent an email to everyone with whom I normally corresponded, letting them know I would not be reading any emails sent while I was out. I informed them of Bill's and my agreement on how business would be run for now. These few items were all I could do in my first four-hour day back at work.

On my way out, I went by Trish's desk and gave her a list of people with whom I needed to meet. I asked her to set meetings up—no more than two per day, and no more than forty-five minutes each. She was happy to do so. I said goodbye and left, beginning my hour-and-fifteen-minute commute back home.

The trip was uneventful, but tiring. Each leg (from bus to train to bus, then walking to my apartment) seemed inexplicably long and mentally torturous. I got home exhausted, defeated, and no less terrified. I fell into bed at 3:30 p.m. without even eating, dreading getting up in the morning and doing it all again.

My second alarm in over three months went off Tuesday morning. (I had awakened before my alarm on Monday.) It was like a steel spike stabbing through my brain. At first, I didn't know what to do. I lunged toward the sound, looking at my alarm clock for a clue as to what was going on. Then, slowly, I became conscious enough to turn off the horrid sound, fall back, and ponder the impossibility of getting out of bed and ready for work.

I called Trish, saying I would be using one hour of vacation leave (all my sick leave had been used in March), and I'd be at work from eleven to two. I managed to reset the alarm for eight. When it went off again, I felt slightly less horrible, and managed to get up and out the door in time for my adjusted start time.

The rest of the week and most of the next were filled with the meetings Trish had set up. They were intended to catch me up on what had occurred in my absence. These meetings and reading and answering emails were what I did four hours per day. My life outside of work was spent preparing to work, getting to work and back home, and recovering from work. I was weary 100 percent of the time. During the weekend, all I could do was sleep. I had no energy to visit with friends, go to the store, cook for myself, and almost no energy to even eat. All but a few of my free hours per day were spent resting. By Sunday evening, I finally felt almost human again, but then the cycle would begin again, and it would be another week before I'd feel anything but exhaustion.

Most of the time, I really and fully realized the impacts of
the stroke to my life. I totally accepted the cognitive issues would
always remain; I'd never drive again, and only time would tell if I
could or could not do my job. This was what I had to work with
forever. Nothing was going to change substantially except how I
dealt with it.

But somehow, in the back of my mind somewhere, lived a vestige
of life the way it had been, and it still shocked and surprised me on
the occasions when I realized the old life was gone. It was like losing
a loved one to death. You know they are gone, but every now and
then, you think, "Oh wow! I can't wait to tell this to Grandma!" and
then you remember you will never talk to Grandma, as you knew
her, again. But in that instance, you have proof-positive Grandma
is gone. I did not have iron-clad proof. Yet.

At my first appointment, my neurologist ordered neuropsychological testing to be done. The earliest testing appointment available was mid-June.

As the date neared, I was excited to get some information on what was going on in my noggin. I arranged rides to and from, as it was a five-hour day, and I didn't want to make it eight with bus commutes. Jennie, my friend who had taken me to work the first day, dropped me off with a "Knock 'em dead, kiddo!" and a pat on the shoulder before I exited her car.

I signed in and waited to be called, wondering what on earth a neuropsychological test entailed. I envisioned wires hooked up to my brain, and Gene Wilder from *Young Frankenstein* holding a clipboard while asking me hilarious questions.

I was shown to a tiny office with a medium-sized, metal desk in it. There were typical doctor's office pictures of people who were transparent so you could see their brains and nerves. These were the only clues the office didn't belong to a low-level clerk. A young man in a slightly too-large white lab coat was seated behind the desk and introduced himself as Doctor Weirman. He looked nothing like Gene Wilder, but rather like a high school student playing dress-up in his dad's clothes.

He was very nice and explained to me how the day would be organized. We would be testing for four hours, with an hour break in the middle. There were no other breaks, so I should go to the restroom before we got started. I had already gone—I grew up driving across Texas with my Mom saying, "Go before we leave, because we aren't stopping until we get there!" so I knew my bladder would be fine for two hours. My brain, however, might be another matter.

Portions of the test were comprised of Dr. Weirman reading information to me and I needed to respond with information I already knew. Examples included naming all the animals in the zoo I could think of in one minute, or all the things that are green, or start with the letter R. These were easy for me—precisely as they would've been before the stroke. I felt completely comfortable and responded effortlessly. I thought this test was going to be a breeze.

Next came questions where the young doctor told me some facts and I had to draw conclusions about complex stories/ideas, and then report the answer to him. The stories were like little mysteries to be solved—similar to word problems in Algebra, but not mathematical. I had loved word problems in high school, but these exercises seemed more difficult. They were more challenging than I thought they should have been. I felt I was getting the correct answers, it simply took me a long while.

There were also portions of the test where he showed me a picture, or something I had to read, and I had to make some response. These were impossibly arduous. I would be shown a complex, abstract shape briefly. Then I'd be shown a different slip of paper with three shapes, and I had to pick out which was the original shape I'd seen. At first, I honestly couldn't do it at all. My brain could not store the images even for the two seconds it took to change the page to the answer sheet. I could not remember what I'd seen when the picture was taken away. Then I discovered I could describe the picture to myself. "It looks like five steps of a spiral staircase that go counterclockwise." Then I could pick it out of the next lineup. The three shapes on the answer sheet looked nothing like each other, so the description didn't have to be insanely detailed. I could now find the answer, not because I remembered how the shape looked, but because I could compare each of the shapes to my verbal description and eliminate those that did not match. This was time-consuming, but I was happy with my problem-solving skills.

There was also an exercise where I got to see a person's face from the front, and then I had to pick which was the same person from side-views of three people. This was excruciating. Luckily, I got to see the first face while I attempted to pick it from a different angle. It was impossible until I used words again. I would look at the face straight on and see the person had a prominent nose, so I could rule out all silhouettes with small noses. If this didn't complete the exercise, I'd pick another feature and do the same until I narrowed it to one person. Of course, it took a ridiculously long time, but I felt success in the fact I could do it at all.

Another exercise was a piece of paper with random numbers typed on it. I was told to circle every "6" on the page. The task was incredibly demanding. As I'd experienced before, it was impossible for me to skim information. I had to look at each and every number and ask myself, "Is that a six?" then move to the next number. I could feel the doctor looking at me as I painstakingly made my way through the hundreds of numerals on the page. I didn't realize how slow I was until he remarked on it when I finished.

When all the testing was complete, I went and lay in the grass near where my ride was picking me up. I was completely depleted—emotionally exhausted and mentally fatigued. I was even physically tired and hadn't done anything physical. More importantly, I felt humiliated, dejected, and devastated. How could some of those tests have been so difficult? My brain had forsaken me.

I wouldn't have results for a couple of weeks. In the meantime, I tried not to think about what this meant. Every day at work was a test as well. A test of my ability to read. A test of ability to understand complex ideas. A test of my stamina. And my performance on the tests at work was as frustrating as my performance had been on the neuropsychological test.

In two weeks, I went back to the little office to receive the test results from Dr. Weirman. His assessment was, while I was quite intelligent, and had scored way above average on some portions of the test, I had failed miserably at others. He said I was, and would always be, "slow, inaccurate and easily tired by many cognitive, especially visual, tasks." Although the news was not unexpected, it was still painful to hear, and I was forced to try to incorporate this information into my newly forming vision of myself—moving forward slowly, inaccurately, and tiredly.

Even with these test results, the tiniest vestige of hope remained that thought, *maybe,* one day, I *might* be able to return to doing my job. But one evening, I was struck full-force with the finality of my situation.

It was the sudden memory of my plans for retirement that brought this epiphany. I had dared to hope for a way to quit my job by age fifty, and to find a way to still earn my retirement. This was the idea I had told myself I would explore while in Costa Rica. Was this how the Universe was fulfilling this hope? Sure, my pension representative had mentioned a disability retirement. I'd toyed with the idea that I might get an earlier retirement approved because of my stroke. I'd even thought about how meaningful it was when all the milestones lined up exactly right, and I'd known I was on this Path for a purpose. But I had never really and completely believed it was an absolute truth that I wouldn't be able to do my job as I had done it before.

That truth now became very real to me. As I sat in my little apartment, I looked up into the eyes of Buddha in my beautiful painting, and there was suddenly certainty. Indeed, I had manifested this, and it was my ordained Path to walk on. Although it was not the answer I would have hoped for, it *was* the answer to my prayers.

With a new resolve, I sent the results of the neuropsychological test to my pension representative and started the conversation about what it takes to receive approval for a disability retirement. I was told the "maximum medical improvement," or time they considered ample for a person who had a stroke to heal, was one year. This meant I would not be eligible to have my case reviewed until one year from the date of my stroke. I would spend at least another eight and a half months at work, but unable to do my job.

I contemplated the meaning of all of this. I admitted to myself not only did I not think I'd ever be able to do my job again, I did not think it was healthy to even try any longer. According to my neurologist, stress was the only "typical" contributing factor to a stroke I had. My research told me once a person has a stroke, they are 25 percent more likely to have another than someone who has not had a stroke. These facts led me to believe I should not work in a stressful environment, under any circumstances.

I had never dealt well with stress, and my job had become a seething, vibrantly colored, spewing bucket of stress, served up in heaping gallons every minute of every day. As much as I loved the organization, the people I worked with, and being a part of my work community, I knew it was poison for me to be there. I knew with 100 percent certainty, leaving my job was the next step along my Path.

I requested, and received, a meeting with my boss and the head of the division's office of human resources. After the formality of greetings, I said bluntly, "I cannot do this job any longer. I know it has only been a month, but it is obvious to me this is bad for my health."

Both Bill and Susan, the HR director, were briefly speechless. I wasn't sure what they had been expecting, but it was not this. Once she gathered her wits, Susan replied, "Well, what does that mean for your job?"

"I am hampering my office by working in a half-time capacity now and knowing I won't return to full functionality means it is not worth the strain on me or the unit to continue. But it will be a year from my stroke before our pension can decide about my retirement. I would like to move out of my position and allow it to be filled. I will need something to do for the next eight months or so, to be productive and earn my keep."

Again, they were both stunned into silence. When the HR director gets involved in a medical leave case, it is ordinarily because the supervisor of the person on leave is trying to get rid of the employee. The person is not being productive and their lack of ability to do the job is negatively affecting the work group.

The person being forced out is usually resistant for many reasons: they cannot afford to move to another (lower-paying) position; they believe they will return to full capability; or they (which is frequently the feeling of the supervisor, but not necessarily true) are "milking" the system. Often, the boss wants to force the person into doing what I was *volunteering* to do.

I noticed Bill had not spoken a word since the meeting started, which was peculiar. He didn't usually let much go on without registering his opinion. I thought perhaps he had been told to keep quiet since he had a penchant for saying the wrong thing, as he did in our first meeting when he asked if I was still "able to think."

I saw a look pass between them that I interpreted as meaning, "Wow, this was easy! Let's get this process started!" But Susan knew to proceed carefully and, I liked to think, was being deferential to my previous years of service and contributions.

"Of course, we want to support you in any way possible during your recovery. We will be happy to make any changes necessary to keep you productive and comfortable over the next year," Susan said. "We will wait for you to figure out what job you can do and tell us what you want."

Then, the meeting was ended, and I was left wondering how I could possibly figure anything out. I had told them I couldn't even do my job. My whole life was in upheaval, and I was giving up a career I'd worked toward for twenty-three years. I felt strangely empowered, yet desperately scared at the same time. And tired. So very, very tired. I had not ever been this tired in my life.

I pondered the outcome of the meeting throughout my workday, and before leaving, I sent an email to Susan and Bill, thanking them for the meeting and asking to be allowed to continue in the fashion I had been going—with someone else handling the day-to-day work and me acting in an advisory capacity—until I could figure out what I would be good at. I would find how to best support the organization while taking care of myself. I was told this arrangement was acceptable, and to check back in any time with any ideas I might have.

Over the next several days at work, I spent a few moments of each task wondering how this could transfer to a new position that matched my capabilities. Someone asked me how to use a certain funding source with very restrictive requirements, and I'd answer, then gather the topic into a mental list. A little later, I had a meeting about how indirect costs were calculated, and ideas for making the process more understandable. Another topic was created for the list. On another day, I was approached about how changing funding levels would affect performance measures.

I spent the last hour of my shift Friday writing down my mental list and musing about how I could combine these into a new job. I knew everything about the organization's very complex finances. I knew a lot about the rules, regulations, policies, and procedures that guided all business aspects of the division. But I couldn't deal well with email, and I couldn't read reports and other information easily. I was unable to handle complexity, even if presented verbally, but I could use the information that was already contained in my brain, and I could advise on the independent details of a complex situation. I had the idea I could sit in the hall with a big sign around my neck that said, "Finance advice given here," like Lucy in the *Peanuts* cartoon with her psychiatric advice. I smirked at the idea. It was not an ideal answer for the organization, but it sparked an idea of something I *could* do.

I formulated a plan whereby I could work in the performance measurement group. This work used to be housed in my office, therefore I knew a lot about it, and it used lots of financial information. It was a highly-complicated model, but had various modules I could work with independently, if someone else were overseeing the big picture. I approached the leader of the group, and he said he would be happy to have me. I thought perhaps I could do this for eight months.

I worked with human resources and we wrote a job description and had it evaluated for classification. WI was a big company, and personnel issues there were known for moving with painstaking slowness, but this process moved insanely quickly. In less than a month, my new position was approved, classified, and office space found for me. I moved my belongings from my big executive office to my new shared cube in the basement and reported to my new boss.

It was weird still being at the same organization but in such a different capacity. I used to supervise a unit of fifty people. Now I was in a unit of six, and not the boss of anyone. I was quickly feeling irrelevant. That stung a bit, but I resolved to get past it. It would be easier if I were gone, not watching myself becoming unnecessary, arcane, obsolete. Bearing witness to this process was the difficult part. But it was not the most difficult thing I'd done during the year, or even during the week. I would be as useful as I could, while protecting my health and staying focused on the work, not the dynamics going on around me.

I had not worked in a cubicle since the '90s. I noted this one was much nicer than my last cubby. Before, I'd had a centuries-old metal desk, a vax terminal (precursor to desktop computers), and a horribly uncomfortable chair.

Today, I had a modular desk, with a fairly new computer. I had been allowed to bring my special chair, bought to accommodate my five-foot-one-inch frame. It was the best chair I'd had in my professional life. I sat back in it, closed my eyes, and took a deep breath. I held it for a few seconds, then exhaled slowly, relaxing noticeably. There, in a small corner of my heart, I could feel my gratitude growing. What did I have to be sad about? I reminded myself all I had loved about the budget director job was dead for me. It died on March 1, when a small part of my brain suffocated. I was grateful the job had died for me before it killed me. As I opened my eyes, I noted I even had a window office! Never mind that the view was bricks inside a four-foot window well, and some weeds therein. I could see sunlight, which was a positive.

In this lower-level position, I still found myself continuously exhausted by work. I went to see my doctor, and she changed my FML orders to say I could only work forty-percent time. I changed my schedule to work four-hour shifts on Monday, Tuesday, Thursday, and Friday, and took Wednesday to rest. The change took effect immediately and the extra twenty-four hours to recharge midweek made such an amazing difference. I could function in my off-hours now. Life seemed to be coming together wonderfully.

I filled my non-work time with getting plenty of sleep, seeing friends, and doing yoga. It was interesting to note again that although working four hours at a job reading, coordinating information, and looking at graphs was absolutely exhausting, doing a ninety-minute, incredibly challenging yoga class, or walking four miles, was not tiring in the least. In fact, it made me feel better. With my reduced work schedule, I had the time and energy to be more active. I could now return to adjusting to my new "normal" and pass the time until I could get information from my pension regarding the rest of my life.

For the most part, my life had become a reasonably predictable pattern. But on occasion, I overdid work, or didn't get proper sleep, and I'd get the exhaustion spells again—or if I only overdid it a bit, the crying spells. In these times, I was again forced to acknowledge the one area where my life was lacking. I yearned for someone who would hold me, love me, care for me. I wanted someone to be there for me. I wanted a partner with whom I could share my life—in sickness or health.

I thought of what Giovanna had said about finding someone who was kind and loving, and my issues wouldn't seem like baggage to him. I was in a lot better place emotionally than I had been when I felt my baggage was insurmountable. I had some idea of what was going to happen to me, I had regained my independence, and I was certain of the long-term effects of the stroke, so why not? Even though I had sworn in the past I'd never do it again, I joined an online dating site.

To manage my energy for work, I couldn't spend much time on the internet, searching for the perfect mate. Instead of actively looking for someone I found interesting, I waited for men to contact me. When they did, I didn't do hours of research, as I had in previous forays into online dating. Instead, I spoke with them right away, and trusted the Universe would eventually bring me the right man through this awkward process. I needed to set boundaries for myself that kept me from getting too exhausted, and trusting the Universe seemed the best way to begin.

As for my baggage, I decided I would not be disingenuous or dishonest, but I would try not to mention my stroke or issues associated with it until I met with my potential mate in person. I wanted them to see how I operated in the world before they judged me for my disability.

The first person I met online was someone who told me he was very health-conscious, but had started having heart attacks in his thirties, and continued to have one every few years. This was terrifying to me, but at least I knew he would certainly accept my health issues. I felt comfortable sharing with him the information about my stroke right away, and he accepted it with no concerns. We talked on the phone quite a bit and had very nice conversations, but, when it came time to meet in person, he kept delaying and became hostile. I decided he wasn't the one. I was grateful for the experience of telling a stranger, a prospective date, about my stroke and associated issues without rejection. The experience with this man had made my condition seem much more acceptable. I moved on to the next promising candidate.

The next man with whom I was matched seemed amazing. He was active and healthy, his pictures were attractive, and we seemed to have a lot in common. We were having some great exchanges, and our conversations started turning toward when we would meet in person. He was staying at a friend's cabin in the mountains for the weekend—a short drive from where I lived—and invited me to come up for the day and go canoeing on the lake nearby. I had to tell him, although I would be excited to go canoeing, I was unable to drive, and therefore, unable to get to his location. When he asked why I could not drive, I told him about my stroke, and he seemed understanding about it. After we hung up, I never heard from him again. He was not the one, either.

I had been conversing sporadically with another man who seemed quite nice. He was now the only candidate in my online dating queue, and as my time was becoming freed up from other suitors, he seemed to become more interested in me. He soon suggested we meet in person, but it was a few weeks before my sister was getting married in Tennessee. At work, I had some deadlines I needed to cover before I could go on vacation, so I knew work would demand all the energy I could give before I left. I did not want to overtax myself, so I told him I was going to need to wait until I got back from the wedding. We had three more weeks to visit via email, and I enjoyed getting to know this guy named Steve.

We had a rally of emails one Saturday where we exchanged short messages every couple of hours. Then, in the early afternoon, he sent a message with a question I could not answer without either being deceitful or telling him about the stroke. I bolstered myself for rejection and told him about my disability. I didn't hear from him again for the rest of the day and became convinced I never would. The next morning, Steve wrote back saying the news was shocking, but he supposed I was the same person he'd liked and enjoyed getting to know, so he suggested we should go ahead and meet. I was relieved to hear from him and wanted to meet him as soon as possible. We set the day for our meeting for a week after my return, on August seventh—it couldn't come fast enough for me.

After attending my sister's wedding, I returned home, and plunged back into work. Then suddenly, it was August seventh, the night for my date. I was very excited to meet Steve. We met for dinner on a Wednesday, my day off, at a place that was easily accessible for me.

I got to the restaurant early and awaited his arrival. As I anticipated his entrance, I suddenly realized I had no idea what he looked like. I needed to see someone several times, and from several angles, before I could develop facial recognition. I had intended to bring a printout of his profile page, which had his picture, but had forgotten it at home. Even with the picture, I wasn't certain I would have recognized him, but I would have had a chance.

I seated myself right in front of the door and waited for someone who looked as if he were searching for his date. Whenever a male entered the restaurant alone and looked around, I smiled and acted as if I recognized him, hoping if he were Steve, he would recognize me and make contact. The first several men I encountered, who were obviously not Steve, seemed a little curious at my knowing looks.

When Steve did make his entrance, I was very surprised. Although a later review of his profile told me he looked exactly like his picture, I recognized him as my date no more than the other three men whom I'd pretended to know. I noted he looked very much like the comedian with whom I had been infatuated right after my stroke. This, and the fact of our long correspondence via email, made me feel more comfortable with Steve, and we seemed to slip right into familiarity.

We had a very pleasant evening and were mutually attracted to one another. He worked in customer service at a firm that provides retirement plans for many large employers. I said I might have even talked to him when I closed out one of my 401ks. We talked about a variety of things, then, when we'd developed a comfort level, the conversation turned to my stroke.

"I know strokes affect people differently, depending on what part of the brain is damaged. You have no obvious signs, but you said you have vision problems. So what part of your brain was injured?"

It was the most insightful question I had received about my experience, and I answered openly, commenting on how much he knew about the topic.

"Well, I don't just know that stuff," he admitted, "I bought *Strokes for Dummies,* so I could understand what was going on and be able to talk somewhat knowledgeably about it."

I was astounded, and excited at his thoughtfulness. It was as if my issues from the stroke were not baggage to him at all! I was glad I had listened to my therapist and decided to try dating, and I was glad I was trying it with this man.

When we finished dinner, he insisted upon picking up the tab, which I genuinely appreciated. We walked out into the parking lot to part ways and realized we wanted more time together. "How about an after-dinner coffee?" he asked.

We walked to a coffee shop down the road. We had coffee and split a piece of pie and talked about our children. His oldest son, Kevin, was heading off to college in a few weeks, and his youngest, Scott, was a junior in high school. He wasn't much for bragging, but I gathered they were athletic and smart. I told him about Jake and Megan.

"I enjoy spending time with my boys, but they are getting to the age where they don't need me much anymore," Steve said. "I decided it was time to start dating to develop another focus in my life, so they can feel free to become independent of me."

We finished our dessert and he let me pick up the small tab. As we were walking back to the first restaurant, where we had had dinner, he said, "You know, I could have driven us over, if you liked."

"Oh my gosh! I didn't even think of driving. I guess I'm used to walking everywhere."

"I figured you were uncomfortable getting into a car with a man you didn't know well, so I didn't say anything."

"You're very considerate, but it wasn't the case at all," I remarked.

"How will you get home?"

"I'll take the light rail to a bus."

"I would be happy to drive you home, if you like."

"Oh, no, I couldn't ask you to do that." I knew he lived in completely the opposite direction from my home, and he had to be at work early in the morning.

"Well, I could at least give you a ride to the train station, then. Would that be alright?"

I agreed. On the short drive, we decided we would like to see one another again soon. I instructed him to pull up into the drop-off lane and let me out near the station entrance, but he surprised me by parking, insisting on walking me down to where the trains came in. Once we got to the tracks, I assumed he would leave, but he waited with me until the train arrived, gave me a hug, and said, "Please text me when you get home, so I know you made it safely."

I was again impressed. The men I had dated since my divorce had not led me to expect this chivalry. I wondered if it were because they were clods or because I was too forcefully independent. Whatever it was, I thought, I could get used to this.

The next weekend, we went out again. Steve suggested lunch and a trip to the horse-racing track, and I loved how he had unique ideas for entertainment. Following dates included a wine festival in the foothills and a picnic—both very romantic and his ideas!

As we got to know one another better, it seemed we were more compatible than we would have been prior to the stroke. Before, I had been insanely active, and would not have even thought of dating someone who was not comparably energetic. Steve was a lot more subdued than I and would have found me way too frenetic. In addition, I was now aware of other aspects of a personality that might be more important than physical activity. Suddenly, characteristics such as kindness, attentiveness, and a loving nature were more of a priority than being able to run five miles or do a downward-facing dog.

Steve had a calmness about him that I found completely soothing, and he had a way of making things seem simpler. He easily accommodated the less stressful lifestyle to which I was aspiring.

In time, I saw a gruffer side of him, too. But having recently experienced being truly vulnerable for the first time in my life, I recognized his standoffishness as discomfort. He struggled with the vulnerability necessary to develop a new partnership. I found cajoling him out of his sternness brought us back to equilibrium. One such instance occurred at his home, as we sat on his huge sectional couch. The segments for sitting were extra-large for one person, but not really built for two. After an hour or so of us each sitting in our own segments, I would ask him to scootch over and let me sit next to him. It was snug, and I had to nestle underneath his arm for us to both fit. It was cozy and lovely.

Sometimes, when I asked to come snuggle with him, he acted grumpy about it, making a slightly frowny face, and saying, "What? There's not enough room."

I would counter, continuing to move in next to him, "Oh, you know you like it. Scoot!"

He would move over and snuggle sweetly with me. On occasion, I got involved in what was on television and didn't make my trek over to his territory of the couch. He confirmed my suspicions that he feigned not wanting me there. "Aren't you going to come visit me?" he said, pressing against the arm of the couch and making room for me next to him.

Pre-stroke Laurie would have been angry with his feigning disinterest in snuggling, not even investigating the source. I would've never understood the discomfort of trying to be vulnerable in a new relationship, because I had never tried to be vulnerable. I would have broken up right away, not understanding (or even trying to understand) his emotions.

Yes, the stroke itself had not only made us more compatible but made the relationship possible. There were many ways my relationship with Steve seemed to be manifested by my long-term and recent desires. He didn't see my having had a stroke or inability to drive as detractors at all. In addition, he fulfilled my wish list by having NFL Ticket! Exactly as I had predicted, even though I had been kidding with my co-worker when I said it. I was quite happy I had added "sweet, compassionate, and loves to cuddle with me" to my wish list, as he had all those traits as well. I enjoyed them immensely.

As I have mentioned, he was not the "perfect soulmate" I'd *thought* I'd wanted—he didn't enjoy physical fitness activities the way I did. (In fact, he could barely bring himself to suffer through workouts at the gym.) Where I was a very healthy eater, he was not really concerned with nutrition or the healthiness of meals and enjoyed very few of the vegetables I loved so much. And he was frequently more pessimistic and less social than I.

In the end, there was a balance we struck with each other. Being around me encouraged him to eat a bit more healthily and become a bit more active. Being around him showed me how to relax and enjoy what was going on in the moment. There was something about being with him that made me happy and whispered to me about how this was the right relationship for me. Accordingly, our relationship blossomed very quickly. In October, within two months of our first date, we were solidly classifying ourselves as a couple.

For my birthday in November, he sent me fifty yellow roses at work, with a note saying, "One for each year of your beautiful life." I felt cared for and loved in a way I hadn't experienced before. My post-stroke life was full of gratitude, and my gratitude for this big, sweet, cuddly man, who was so different from me, was becoming boundless.

In January, as I approached the one-year anniversary of the stroke, I became uneasy. I now knew, with certainty, that I could not go back to a full-time desk job with my impairment. I wondered what would happen if I weren't approved for the disability retirement. I would need a way to support myself that didn't exhaust me or put my health in danger. I began running through the options in my mind.

I knew it would have to be more of a physical, rather than heavily cerebral job. I could do massage, but after my last experience as a massage therapist, I had a more realistic idea of what seemed financially (and physically) possible for me in that line of work. It would be a good, part-time base income, but I would need more if my retirement were not approved.

I had been a great cocktail waitress in my youth and had enjoyed the job. Could I be a server again? It seemed my problems with facial recognition and spatial relations would likely hinder me. It was great to fill your tray with beers and cocktails, but if you couldn't recognize from whom you'd taken the order, or remember where their table was located, that would be problematic.

What about yoga? Maybe I could become a yoga teacher. There was a teacher training coming up at the end of February in the studio where I practiced. It was a definite possibility. A career in yoga would go well with massage, too. I had loved yoga for many years but had never been interested in teaching it. I felt I loved it too much to make it into a job. But in my desperation, I grasped at anything that could help me be financially solvent if things didn't work out as I hoped they would.

I explored every idea I could imagine. As January dragged on, I became more and more frightened of what might happen to me if I couldn't retire and hadn't figured out a way to support myself.

I called Mom and discussed my fears. I told her I had money saved up. I had sold my two rental properties and put the money away. This money would get me by for quite a while, but I needed a fallback plan. If all else failed, I asked, could I move in with her and my stepdad? It was a tough question to think, much less to ask. I hadn't lived with them since I was seventeen. She said yes (of course), and I felt a little more at ease.

That evening, I told Steve about the conversation. I had mentioned my fears to him before, but I had minimized them, not believing our relationship was advanced enough to expect his help with these problems.

"You're thinking of moving to Alabama?" he said, with his brow furrowed.

"Well, only in the direst of circumstances," I answered.

"I think we can come up with a better solution," he said, putting on his grumpy, "I'm hiding my feelings from you" face that indicated he was stepping out of his comfort zone to assure me.

Normally, this would be where I would tease him into admitting his feelings, but I was feeling a bit vulnerable too, so I said, "Do you mean you would help me?"

His voice turned tender, as he saw the look of love and fear on my face. "Yes, of course I would help you. I need to keep you here, with me."

I swooned and felt even more greatly assured and comfortable. I had felt our relationship was heading toward moving in together eventually, so we simply had the conversation early. Everything was going to be okay.

By mid-January, I decided to enroll in yoga teacher training. The training would end in early April, perhaps about the time I would learn of my pension's decision about my retirement. If I received the retirement, I could still consider teaching yoga, and if I were denied, I could start right away. I contacted the yoga teacher program I was considering and met with the manager to find out how demanding it was. The answer was, quite demanding. There was a good deal of reading, plus class several times a week, in the evenings and on Saturdays. There was no way I could do the training, work part-time, and remain healthy, or even sane.

Then an idea, which had unknowingly been simmering on the back burner, bubbled to the forefront of my mind. I could go on hiatus from work and have enough vacation time, at sixteen hours per week, to cover me for a couple of months. Being on leave, I would still get my reduced paycheck, short-term disability check, and have benefits—and therefore a safety net—with freedom to explore these other options.

I was torn about how to proceed and looked desperately for a sign to assure me this was the right course of action. I had some oracle cards, like cards used for tarot readings, or "fortunetelling." Looking for a sign, I pulled them out, and as a lark, I put them against my heart and whispered, "What should I do about work and this new plan?"

As I shuffled through the cards, one seemingly threw itself from the deck. I picked it up, and I had my answer. "Take a leap of faith," the card told me.

I put the plan into motion. I wrote up my notice and met with my supervisor. Last February 28 had been my last day as a full-time WI employee due to the stroke. February 28 this year was my last day at work as a part-time employee.

My first step was becoming a massage therapist again. I knew I couldn't depend upon it for my entire income, but it would be a start, and something I could do right away. I applied for a massage therapist position at the wellness center where I'd worked before—which, "coincidentally," was within walking distance of my apartment. I got the job, with a start date of March 2.

I enrolled in yoga teacher training and committed to finding a way to enjoy doing yoga as a pastime and a job. I didn't know if this combination would provide enough money, but I was certain it would take me to my limits physically.

I had Steve's offer of help as my fallback, but his emotional support was even more important. With him in my corner, I assuaged my anxiety and managed to live in the moment. His favorite saying to me was, "You're overthinkin' it," and indeed, I had been overthinking everything for many years.

I had lots of options, which I would phase in gradually, after I received the decision from my pension. If they denied me, I could start layering on the options until I was able to support myself: massage therapist, yoga teacher, and/or move in with Steve.

If my retirement were approved, nothing was wasted. I would likely want a part-time job anyway, and massage was perfect. I wouldn't need to do anything more to support myself. And, I would have learned great things in yoga teacher training, which I could use for my own wisdom, or to teach, if I so chose.

After my last day of work, there was a big happy hour in my honor. Co-workers came and went, and there were around fifty people there at any time. All the managers I had worked with in my position as Budget Director were there. I hadn't seen most of them since I'd moved to the basement, but it was nice to see them now.

And Steve was there, by my side, meeting everyone and showing he was a part of my new life. After everyone left, he walked me back to my apartment, barely a block away. He had a bottle of champagne, and we toasted to the end of my old life and the beginning of my new one.

On March 1, I took the day for a time of introspection. I woke up and read the journal I'd been writing since Aunt Sherry had suggested it a little less than a year ago. I thought about the changes in my life, and how I was handling them. I cried a little and celebrated a little.

Then, I called my pension representative, as she had said they would be able to decide about my future after a year had passed. It was likely she wouldn't have an answer yet, but I wanted to remind her it had been a year. She said she needed more information from my doctors, forms filled out, my tax return from the previous year. After she got what she needed, she would schedule a meeting with the review panel, so I probably wouldn't hear anything for at least another month. I had been prepared for such an answer and was glad I had not waited for this day to make decisions about my future.

I started work at the wellness center the following day. Yoga teacher training had started the week before. I was solidly on the Path to my new life.

I had expected yoga teacher training to be a life-altering experience, like massage school had been. But it was quite anti-climactic. I didn't feel like I had met my Soul's Purpose, or like I had even found something viable for my life. On the last day of training, the instructors planned a small ceremony. As a part of it, each of the students drew a rock from a bag. The rocks had words, designed to be meaningful and prophetic, written on them. Mine had the word "Teacher" on it. I was disappointed with it, and wished I'd received a different word. At the end of the ceremony, I felt nothing, except relief that the demands of the class had ended.

What I did get from the yoga teacher training was a new yoga "home." During the course, we had to attend classes at three places other than the studio where the program was taught. I had been struggling with the place where I was doing yoga, and where I was taking the teacher training program, for some time.

It had worked well for me before the stroke, because I didn't realize my need for a more spiritual practice than I received from the very athletically-driven place I was attending. I had truly loved the place over the years, but I needed something different now.

One of the places I chose to take a class during teacher training turned out to be one of the most moving, loving, spiritual experiences I had encountered since the yoga retreat in Costa Rica. My first class there was heaven-sent. The studio was in an older building and was very simple. They didn't have racks of over-priced retail merchandise, or loud hip-hop music, but instead, a simple desk and soothing yoga chants, which enveloped me as I entered. The person greeting me looked me right in the eyes and seemed genuinely happy to see me. She had a peaceful demeanor and asked how I was doing today, as if she really cared how I was doing.

I filled out the paperwork, grabbed my mat and went into the yoga room. I was the first one there, because the bus that serviced the area could either get me there twenty-five minutes early, or five minutes late.

I looked around the room and detected it had been lovingly remodeled, with beautiful cork-look floors. A sign that said, "Do the kindest things in the kindest ways" rested on the windowsill. There was a small altar table at the front of the room, with a statue of Buddha on it. I felt happy and renewed simply being there. I picked my spot near the right side of the room, so no one would be in my blind area. I settled in to meditate until class started.

Our instructor was Sean, who was famous in the Denver yoga world. He walked in, not looking like the yoga rock star I expected. He was dressed simply in shorts and a T-shirt. He was slim and fit, and handsome, with a boyish grin that spoke of his ability to accept everyone for whomever they were.

The yoga itself was good, and it was well-taught. The dharma talk was simply wonderful. The message was how we all lie to ourselves throughout life, and how to recognize and correct this. I thought about the lies I had told myself earlier in life—about how life needed to be hard. From that day, I committed to seeing through the lies I told myself, and to attending Sean's class regularly.

I was getting off the bus on my way to a yoga class when my phone rang. It was my pension representative. She said the review panel had met about me that morning, April 14, and they had decided I would never be competent to do my pre-stroke job, or any job like it, again. I was approved for retirement.

When I heard those words spoken out loud, when I was called incompetent, I was stunned. Although I had waited for this news for a year, it was as if this were the first time I'd realized I was not going back to my old job. I guess it's the first time I was 100 percent certain. I had a panel of professional opinions now that said it was true. I was officially retired. It was quite surreal. I should have been overcome with excitement—jumping for joy. But I was numb, for the moment.

I texted Steve and told him the news. He replied, "We should celebrate. Where would you like to go to dinner tonight?" I was in the middle of typing a text saying I'd like to have a quiet night at home and do something soothing, like have some wine and a bubble bath. While I was typing this out, but before I hit send, I got a text from Steve saying, "How about if I make a nice dinner at home, open a bottle of wine and draw you a bubble bath?"

Wow, I thought, *I ended up retiring at age fifty and found a man who not only doesn't think I'm baggage, but who also can practically read my mind. I've received everything I asked for. Something so wondrous requires a little processing, I guess.*

I walked to yoga class in a fog, wondering if this were all real. When I got there, I managed to clear my mind and concentrate on my practice. It was a peaceful hour with another one of my favorite teachers, who always had the most amazing messages for me. Nicole's message that day was about accepting change, and how sometimes change is difficult, even if it is positive. Her message seemed designed with me in mind and was exactly what I needed. I left class with a clear mind, still feeling a little surreal, but instead of being in a fog, I was walking on clouds.

That night, sitting in a beautiful bubble bath, drinking a lovely glass of wine while Steve was downstairs making dinner, I thought about Nicole's message. I realized I could make this change as traumatic or as loving as I wished it to seem. I needed to stop thinking of my career as something that had been taken from me, and instead think of retirement as a gift. I succumbed to relief and gratitude. I saw clearly the Path I had traveled over my lifetime, as though the events of my life were beads strung on a thread that led to this moment, where I realized the power and wonder of manifestation.

I remembered a time when I was young, and manifestation was simply something that happened, with no real thought or effort on my part. From a baby brother to a pay increase of exactly $400, I had simply thought about the desire, and it had somehow been provided.

Then came the time when things got hard. I had stopped thinking good things were a part of life and started believing I had to work hard and earn every single good break. Good things continued to happen, but they were far from effortless. The more I believed in hard work, the harder I had to work to get the things I wanted.

The next bead represented the time after my doctor pronounced my need to change my life or die. I knew I was struggling with stress-induced illnesses, but I had tried to brush off these warnings, because of my belief about needing to work harder. But these words, spoken by a doctor whom I respected and trusted, were the exact catalyst I needed. In time, the words moved me enough to eliminate my fear of leaving the job of CFO. Something whispered to me to take the risk, and everything would work out as it should.

Another bead represented when I quit my job and went to massage school. I became a massage therapist for a few very happy years. But then, somehow, I was guided away from massage and back to finance.

There were many instances when I had looked back at leaving massage therapy and been disappointed with myself for quitting before my money ran out. Perhaps, I thought, I had been on the Path to fulfilling my Soul's Purpose, and I had given up—sold out. But in this moment of reflection in the bubble bath, I knew my time as a massage therapist had turned out to be a means to an end. During that time, I learned to allow life to be easy again. I learned to put a name to what I'd done in my youth without knowing I was doing it: manifestation. I had found my spirituality and regained my ability to see the world as a kind and loving place. A place where we take care of each other and the Universe takes care of us. And although I left the world of being a massage therapist to return to my old world, I was forever changed by the experiences I had there.

I recalled the book I wrote while doing massage. First, to have so synchronistically met a writing coach right after I started writing was a wonder. Writing the book had seemed so meaningful at the time, yet it would be ten years before I would fully understand what the experience of writing the other book was to play in my life. It was, in fact, a rehearsal for this memoir, which is much more powerful and meaningful than the tips and tricks I wrote about before.

There was a bead for the time after leaving massage. I found myself a few years later in the *exact* job I'd held before. But I was a different person, and I approached everything in my life in a different manner. I did work hard and take on too much stress, but all the while, I was making plans to retire soon—sooner than anyone would have thought was possible. I allowed myself to have faith things would turn out for the best.

During this time, I changed my lifestyle to live on less money. Interestingly, as soon as I made my unlikely retirement plan, things started falling in place to help me reduce my budget. One example was the friend who needed an investment and refinanced my second mortgage. I thought I was making all these changes to pay for reinstating my pension. In fact, I was learning to simplify my life and get by on less money. The Universe was directing me to a life of ease of which I previously had no concept—a life where I would make less than half as much money but live more richly.

There was a bead for the lessons I learned at my Costa Rican yoga retreat. The most important of these was when Katy had us do the class with our eyes closed. Her compelling dharma talk instructed us in the ways the Universe communicates with us. The message was so powerful and poignant. I knew the Universe had been whispering to me for years, maybe decades, and I knew my health problems were the beginning of the Universe yelling at me.

The yelling got real when, on the *exact* day—not the day before or after—that I became eligible to request a disability retirement, I had a stroke. My entire world was destroyed and recreated in that very instant. Up to this very moment, I had thought I began manifesting the stroke when I decided to retire at age fifty. I now realized I had been manifesting the stroke from the day I started believing life had to be difficult.

It was a hard ending before a new, soft beginning. As this thought came to me in my bath, it startled me. An audible gasp escaped my lips as I saw all the beads of my life strung together. The biggest, most decorative bead of all was right there in the middle—the life-altering day when I was sitting in an ambulance, thinking, *I'm just surviving this moment.*

In that instant, so many things became impossible, yet the possibilities spread before me like the bubbles in my bath. The stroke had forced me to slow down and reassess what life means, and to see the gifts—the blessings—hiding behind the adversity.

My next bead was Steve. I had struggled for years to find the "right" romantic partner and decided I would have even less success after becoming disabled. Yet, if Steve and I had met before the stroke, I doubt either of us would have considered dating the other.

I would not have invoked his thoughtful, considerate, generous aspects, because I hadn't yet learned to allow others to take care of me. He would not have elicited from me the woman who would step back and see the bigger picture of why we belonged together. Together, we are the recipe where you mix two ingredients that seemingly will not work, and you are rewarded with the most refreshing and lovely dish you've ever tasted. We bring out the very best, most romantic, thoughtful characteristics of one another.

I saw the bead signifying the yoga teacher training, which, once I decided not to teach yoga, seemed like a non-event. I now understood the purpose of enrolling was not to make yoga my new career, but to give me a reason to leave my job at WI. It was not to make me a yoga teacher, but to lead me to the Path, and my Soul's Purpose.

The rest of the beads were strung with mystery. They were the future manifestations and events of my life. One of the beads, I hope, denotes seeing this book published, and bringing a message of hope to my readers.

Each bead showed me a blessing, which was found in looking deeper, losing my biases and perceptions about what life should be, and allowing the Universe to bring what I needed; being open to letting go of the life I'd planned, to have the wonderful life that was awaiting me.

Not only was my life touched by the occurrences counted on the beads, but my children, too, have been touched, moved, and changed by the Path I have been put upon.

Although both were legal adults when the stroke hit, our relationship was still one of parent and children. They each struggled with finding their paths to the future and handling independent life. On that day, when they walked over to see me, they looked down at their mom, lying in a hospital bed, with tubes and wires coming out of her in every direction, with monitors beeping and blinking. The experiences of that day and the following three months of my recovery forced them to grasp so much more.

They gazed at someone upon whom they had depended their entire lives, who needed them now more than they had ever needed her. They understood what most children don't understand until their parents are much older than forty-nine—at some point, they become the caretakers, and their parents become the ones who need to be taken care of. They learned to have a strength borne from facing the fallibility of someone to whom they had ascribed immortality.

They learned the confidence that becomes real, when you pretend you believe it when you say, "Shhhhhh…. everything will be okay." They learned to love in a way that one only learns by tending to the needs of another before their own. They took these teachings and put them to use in their lives.

I saw each of them blossom in ways that amazed me. They became more independent, even sometimes forcibly denying my desire to give financial or other motherly assistance. They are now people who appreciate every moment of life and live it to its fullest. They learned to have compassion for those who are disadvantaged, and to champion the rights of those unable to be their own champions.

We all learned, at the end of life, all you really have is your morals and the relationships you have created, and it is no use if those are not strong and remarkable. Jake and Megan are very different in many aspects, but both have been marked in these ways by the experience of not knowing if they were going to lose their mother. And later, learning they did lose her, but she was replaced by a similar, yet better, version of her former self. They are two people who are changing the world for the better every day—merely by who they are. They are the two most extraordinary people I have ever known.

The most powerful blessing of all was learning to be a ship on the ocean. Allowing the good to come to me, without fighting against what I considered to be the bad. I now trusted the Universe, or ocean, to guide me in the direction I needed to go. That trust had been rewarded with the ability to stop working in an environment that was toxic to me. And I had a pension that would provide enough money to live a nice, quiet life. I had the luxury of thinking about what I *chose* to do with my time, instead of allowing a career to be my tyrannical dictator, directing me into an early grave.

And in the blindness from the stroke, my eyes had been opened to see I had been choosing all along—I simply had not recognized how choosing differently could enrich my life so. Here again, I had needed to contemplate beyond the surface of the adversity. The stroke had taken away my career and many abilities. But, in return, I was given freedom and the opportunity to lead a simple, healthy, and happy life.

I sat in the bubble bath, enjoying my glass of wine and listening to soothing music. I knew, as surely as I had manifested all the "lucky" breaks I had had in my youth, I had manifested this stroke, and it was the luckiest break of all.

Astoundingly, everything made sense. I remembered the saying, "It is always darkest before the dawn," a reminder that we are tested throughout life. It seems when we start to get closest to our goals, the Universe asks us, "Do you really want this? Are you really willing to stick with your intentions even when despair is upon you?"

My ultimate manifestation, this literal stroke of luck, had shown me my Soul's Purpose was not to be a budget director, or even a massage therapist. It was not to trudge through life, overwhelmed and under-satisfied, and it was not to make a life alone.

My Soul's Purpose is to be happy every single day with whatever the Universe is giving me; to be a teacher and share my life and my story with those who desire to learn a new way of living; to make a home with the love of my life and live luckily ever after.

Manifesting on Purpose

Beginning when I became a massage therapist, my path brought me many intuitive and insightful friends, who shared their observations with me about what they saw in my life and my actions. These friends shared not only their own thoughts, but also encouraged me to explore new ideas. In this endeavor, I found books and information that helped me to understand how the Universe was designed to work with, and for, each of us.

I am still learning about manifestation, and refining what I know is possible. I now manifest things in a more positive way, with fewer costs to pay. I manifested a beautiful home for me and Steve, at a price far below what we had thought we would pay—in a market that was steadily climbing.

I experienced the increase in value of a small piece of real estate I had purchased, which far exceeded even the most optimistic market estimates. And I, with a brain that finds it difficult to read, compare complex ideas, and organize information, wrote this book over the course of two years, from a journal that my aunt happened to mention would be a good idea for me to keep.

These events have been filled with what many call coincidence, but what I know to be signs I am moving in the right direction—I am on the Path. My current Soul's Purpose is to share this information on how to be a powerful and fearless manifestor—with you.

Perhaps you cannot quite get yourself to believe completely in the Path or the Soul's Purpose. The signs are all around you, but you cannot see them, right before your eyes. I hope my story gave you an inkling of what is possible and stirred your curiosity to explore these ideas further.

The fact that you have read this book means the stirring has started, and you are beginning down your Path. Your steps on the Path will differ from mine and the Path of others, but you will learn to know when they are heading in the right direction.

As you start to pay attention, you will see the signs that direct you. These signs include a strong intuition telling you a certain action is right (regardless of logic); a series of coincidences that lead to a desirable outcome; and a deeply moving happiness. They will not appear to you overnight but will start with a trickle. The more you notice, the more apparent the clues become, and soon they will be an everyday part of your life.

I have used manifestation all my life—unknowingly and haphazardly—with good, but out-of-control results. As I wrote this book, I formalized a process for manifesting the things I desire in my life. Through refinement and development of the process, abundance has flowed more frequently, and my results have been more pleasant to receive. The process is not a step-by-step manual, but rather a set of practices, to be used on a regular, if not daily, basis.

Meditation

If you do nothing else, meditation will lead you slowly and surely to the answers you desire. I have investigated and studied many kinds of meditation: attention to breath, chakra, intuitive visioning, Neurosculpting®, and guided meditations in many different flavors. You name it, I tried it. There was not one single method that I found a waste of my time. I still alternate between several different versions, depending on how I feel any particular day. But no matter what type of meditation I do, it is my top priority for the day, meditating a minimum of five days a week.

You should try as many forms as you like, giving each at least a month before you move to the next. Take bits you like from one and combine them with bits you like from another. Or, find one and stick to it without straying. As one of my favorite yoga teachers says, "The best kind of meditation is the kind you do."

Meditation is important because it teaches you how to use your brain in a different way; it teaches you how to pay attention and be in the present moment. But meditation is most important because it connects you to the Universe.

A very religious friend once asked me about the difference between prayer and meditation, and I told him, "Prayer is when you talk to God. Meditation is when you let God talk to you." These are the truest words I have ever spoken.

Set Intentions

Manifestation starts when you set intentions for what you want in life. You probably already have these. They are wishes, hopes, and dreams, but turning them into intentions formalizes them. You may write them down, put them on a vision board, draw them in a sketchpad, or simply hold them in your heart.

You need to have conviction that an intention is, in some unknown way, possible. But intentions need not be logical to attain, at the moment you make them. For instance, at forty-nine, I set an intention to retire by age fifty. To me, it was an illogical idea, but I knew it was what I needed, and I had conviction that somehow, it would happen. As you know, it did!

Let Go of Expectations (and Control)

This is probably the hardest part. You cannot control *how* you manifest your intention. The Universe will craft the best outcome for you at the time it comes to fruition. If you try to choose how things will happen, you will be disappointed.

Before I quit my job to be a massage therapist, I hoped I would be able to leave work by winning the lottery. It was the only way I could fathom it happening. But the Universe urged me strongly to move in the direction of becoming a massage therapist. Doing so put me in the right place to learn the things I would need later in my life.

Be assured—if you do stray from the Path, you have not been permanently diverted from, or missed, achieving your desires. The Path will be presented to you repeatedly, whether you believe in it, want it, are aware of it, or not. There are many times I look back on in my life, where I feel I may have stepped off the Path. But the Universe kept redirecting me and giving me opportunities to choose it, again and again. Your Path, too, will be there when you are ready for it.

Look For, and Follow, the Signs

Some signs will be easy to spot, and some a bit harder. When I come upon one now, I know it because I have a stirring in my chest, and a need to pause and reflect on what happened. But when you are first starting, it might not be so easy. Also, I don't always know what the sign means immediately. I simply know it is a sign, and I watch for other things that connect to it.

For instance, when I was working at the grant specialist job, after I had started helping my stepdad work on his grant application, I suddenly saw shoes everywhere. I walked down the street, and I saw a pair of shoes, side by side, next to the sidewalk. It seemed odd, and I noticed them in a way that told me they had meaning. When I went to a meeting the next day and saw a pair of sandals sitting in the conference room, I really took note of the oddity. I asked, and no one knew why the shoes were there. A couple of days later, I found a pair of shoes in my closet that I had been looking for. I thought, *What the heck is the message about shoes?* I couldn't understand the message, so I did an internet search for the meaning of shoes in dreams. The first thing I found was a post saying dreams of shoes can symbolize how one is moving forward on a career or spiritual path. And soon, I had a new job!

The first signs you will see will look like coincidences. There are no coincidences, only unrecognized signs. When something strikes you as coincidental, notice it. Write it down so you can think about it later. Journal on it. And watch for other things that are similar.

Do the Work and Learn the Lessons as You Await Your Outcome

You must do the work necessary to get to the Path and your Soul's Purpose. Sometimes, the work will be mentally and/or physically difficult, but you will know you are on the Path if you feel like you are flowing with your intentions.

I have said repeatedly I know I was not on the Path when life got hard, yet I'm saying you can be on the Path, but the work can be difficult. There is a subtle difference that puts these two concepts worlds apart.

When Scott and I first started Mile High Moving, we definitely did difficult work. He performed four to six complete household moves per day, working with customers who were in the most stressful times of their lives. I answered phone calls, did box-packing jobs, and managed the books and the staff.

The work was physically, emotionally, and intellectually challenging. Yet, we didn't feel beaten down at the end of the day. We felt tired, yet refreshed, and as if we were doing something good. We felt *happy*.

Conversely, when I was working as a CFO, I felt exhausted, drained, and beaten. I felt like Sisyphus from Greek mythology, who was forced to roll a huge boulder up a hill, only to have it roll back to the bottom of the same hill. Then he had to begin the same impossible endeavor, rolling it up the hill, again.

If your life feels Sisyphean, you are not on the Path. If it feels difficult, yet hopeful, then you are probably near, or approaching the Path. But if it feels like you are not working hard at all, or are working hard for a great purpose, and you feel fantastic at the end of the day—like a workout that brings tiredness but an endorphin-filled goodness—then you are *on the Path!*

While you are doing this work, you will have to learn lessons along the way, as I did. The lessons don't have to be hard, like having a stroke. They may be simple, like being in a job you are not fond of long enough to learn a grant application process that helps your stepdad. And, as in this example, the ordained outcome may not be completely obvious. Know it is at work somewhere, leading to a later step along your Path.

Keeping, and periodically reviewing, a journal is very useful in this process. You can look back at things that happened, and how you thought about them. You will gain enlightenment about the teachings you were receiving, and how to use them in the upcoming lessons in your life.

Gratitude

Gratitude works for you in four ways. First, gratitude signals the Universe to give you even more. It shows the Universe you are receiving and appreciating the messages, and you want more.

Second, looking for things to be grateful for illustrates to you exactly what you are receiving. My stroke might have felt like a punishment or worse, had I not been looking for something for which to be grateful. I might have never applied for retirement, and continued to plod along, unable to do my job, and feeling I was cursed. In the end, I would have been fired for not doing my job well, and might have caused myself to have another stroke, or a heart attack. But instead, I found the gift the Universe was giving me, and created a new life that I love more than I would have believed possible.

Once you start to see the trickle of synchronicity, and signs of where the Path is leading, it's very important to express gratitude for what you are receiving, even if it's not *exactly* what you had in mind. Many times, we receive an unexpected influx of money, right before we have a financial hardship. We get $350 the day before the washing machine goes out, and the repair bill is $350. Instead of being angry the extra money was suddenly taken, and did not allow for some indulgence, be grateful for the extra money that kept the washer repair from being a hardship.

When you first start to manifest, you will manifest in this manner. Maybe it happens this way because the Universe is testing you, or sending you signals of abundance. Perhaps it occurs this way because you don't feel worthy of receiving something good.

The third reason to be grateful is that being grateful illustrates how you do, indeed, deserve the gifts the Universe has to offer. It provides a sense of worthiness, so you can manifest things with less ambivalent outcomes.

The fourth thing gratitude does for you is important even if you don't believe (yet) in your ability to manifest the ideal life for yourself. Gratitude creates happiness and the feeling of abundance, even in less desirable circumstances. Right after the stroke, I could only find the strength and wisdom to be grateful I had not died or had a more debilitating stroke. My thankfulness carried me through and quickly generated more gratitude, until I could get to the point of being grateful the Universe had forced me to change from a life that was not serving me well. My gratitude then assuaged my fear and sadness and allowed me to see possibilities.

Cultivate Your Feelings of Worthiness

After meditation, the most important, indeed urgent, work you need to do is find a way to feel worthy of good things in your life. You could start by noticing when your self-talk is devaluing. ("I don't know why I thought I was getting an extra $350 to do something fun. What have I done to deserve it?") When you notice this, correct it by telling yourself you deserve abundance. Try to make this positive self-talk a habit.

You may also realize a sense of worthiness through journaling, meditation, yoga, and therapy. You will find the correct method, and as you develop this sense of worth, things will begin to come more easily, and with fewer prices to pay.

Above, I mentioned feeling gratitude will help you develop self-worth. Developing self-worth will also help you to feel gratitude. When you feel you deserve something good, you will find the good in things and be grateful.

Receive

As the Universe gives to you, you must be able to receive the gifts. Sometimes, a gift is offered by the Universe, and you feel too unworthy, afraid, or simply don't understand the gift, so you decline it. Once you start seeing and following the signs, the gifts will begin to make sense to you. Then you can receive them. Every day I say to myself, "The Universe gives me the things I need. And I accept them. With Gratitude." When you learn to receive the gifts (with gratitude), you will receive more.

Practice

As I said before, this is not a step-by-step process, but rather, a group of practices to be used daily. Each feeds upon the other and doing one will increase your skills at using the rest. It all works together, exactly like the world of nature. Plants use carbon dioxide and produce oxygen, while animals use oxygen and produce carbon dioxide. These are not coincidences. Each cycle completes, and builds upon, another.

Now I know these things, which doesn't mean I'm perfect at recognizing the signs and taking the Path quickly and effortlessly. Nor does it mean I always remember I am worthy of great gifts, received effortlessly (although I get better every single day).

I still buy lottery tickets occasionally, in case the Universe decides it is how I should reach another Soul's Purpose. I seek signs, and I'm sure I sometimes miss them. I'm still struggling with the effects of a single autoimmune disease as I write this, and I'm trying to find the meaning in this remnant of my old life.

I am continuing to do the things that bring me joy and a sense of moving in the right direction. Each day, I do these things more intentionally and with less frustration. I have manifested amazing things throughout my life, and they have been coming more frequently and easily as I have been perfecting these practices. I absolutely know even greater things are in store for me if I continue to take in the lessons I am learning, and this will allow me to prepare for finding my ever-more satisfying Soul's Purpose.

And so, I hope you, my dear reader, can take some solace and encouragement from my travels on the Path, and put them to good use in your quest for your ideal life.

With love and hope,

Laurie

Acknowledgments

Many thanks to the people who made this book possible, for without you, I wouldn't know where to begin telling my story:

My Mom, Madeline, who taught me to be self-reliant, kind, and lady-like (although the lady-like didn't always take). You are a shining example to me, and I love you more than you can know.

My children, Megan and Jake, who had to grow up fast, and learned to appreciate life. The two of you are my inspiration, moral compasses, guidance counselors, and the best friends anyone could ever have. I am entirely amazed at the wondrous humans you have grown up to be and can barely contain my joy at being your mother.

Aunt Sherry, the first feminist I ever knew. You bought me a train set, because you weren't allowed to have one as a little girl, and you showed me that being a woman is not a limitation. As my first live-in caregiver after the stroke, you encouraged me to keep a journal, telling me I never knew what might come of it. Thank you for all your support in my life and this process.

My sister, Beth, who taught me how to have a sense of humor about *everything*, and to understand when there's a choice between laughing and crying, always choose laughter. You have kept everyone laughing through some harrowing times in your life, and you are my hero in so many ways.

My brother, for whom I wished upon a star, Mike. I learned to nurture from taking care of you as a baby. As an adult, you taught me the delicate art of sarcasm, and that love is present, whether you make a big show of it or not.

My "other" brother, Bart. Although we didn't grow up together, I have grown so much from knowing you these last ten years. We had a choice, and we chose to be family.

The hundreds of friends who supported me in my various careers, my stroke recovery, and my post-stroke reinvention of myself. I'm sorry that I can't name you all and tell you individually what you mean to me here—although I hope I have done so in everyday life. The acknowledgements would be longer than the book itself! Every piece of advice, encouraging word, bit of honest feedback, has helped bring me to this moment. I can hardly believe the good fortune I have in the people who have been in my life over these fifty-five years. Bless you all, as you have blessed me so deeply.

My editor, Alexandra O'Connell, who helped make this story into a book. It would be a shell of what it is without your insightful suggestions. Thank you for helping me grow my baby into something beautiful!

My advisor, Susie Schaefer, who kept me on-track. You showed me the path through this crazy process and kept me out of the weeds. I am confident this would never have happened without your diligent assistance and wisdom.

About the Author

Laurie Freedle's retirement at age fifty came at the price of having a stroke, so she went back to the drawing board. In her ensuing journey, she found that she had unknowingly prepared herself spiritually, financially, and physically for the challenges she faced.

Setting out to rebuild her life and reinvent her relationship with manifestation, Laurie turned misfortune into her ideal life. She now touts leisure time, favorable real estate deals, the love of her life, and a career as a speaker and author in her menu of manifestation miracles. Her eclectic background—from cocktail waitress, small business-owner, executive at a billion-dollar company, to massage therapist—has equipped her with the wit and wisdom to entertain and enlighten readers and listeners alike.

Laurie has extensively studied yoga, holistic health, gardening, and manifestation in the lives of others. She lives in Denver, Colorado, with her husband Steve, where she enjoys summers working on their half-acre urban farm, and winters awaiting any opportunity to go to the beach. To book Laurie for an engagement or learn more about her journey, email laurie@lauriefreedle.com.

Dare to Create Your Ideal Life

Laurie Freedle, CEO of Spiritual Audacity LLC, is excited to offer the following:

Personal Appearances and Workshops

- As a special offer to her readers, Laurie will visit your book club, via Skype or in person

- Laurie is available to speak at your event, or do a workshop, on a wide range of topics, including:

  - How to Remain Optimistic in a Pessimistic World

  - Self-Care

  - Stress Management/Reduction

  - Finding Inspiration in Adversity

Neurosculpting Facilitation and Meditation
(Available starting June 2019)

- Neurosculpting is a meditation and education process that helps take the limbic brain off-track in order to oust limiting beliefs and entrain a new, positive story

  - Neurosculpting workshops can be designed on virtually any topic, from manifesting your ideal life, to eliminating fear, or becoming a more creative thinker

  - Neurosculpting guided meditations can be customized and recorded for your personal needs

Website & Blog

- Laurie's blog shares the wisdom that life has to offer us through her witty and insightful posts, visit www.lauriefreedle.com.